THE NEW SCHOOL

The New School

HOW THE INFORMATION AGE
WILL SAVE AMERICAN EDUCATION
FROM ITSELF

GLENN HARLAN REYNOLDS

ENCOUNTER BOOKS

NEW YORK · LONDON

© 2014 by Glenn Harlan Reynolds

First American edition published in 2014 by Encounter Books, an activity of Encounter for Culture and Education, Inc., a nonprofit, tax exempt corporation.
Encounter Books website address: www.encounterbooks.com

Manufactured in the United States and printed on acid-free paper. The paper used in this publication meets the minimum requirements of ANSI/NISO 39.48–1992 (R 1997) (*Permanence of Paper*).

FIRST AMERICAN EDITION

LIBRARY OF CONGRESS CATALOGING-IN-PUBLICATION DATA

Reynolds, Glenn H.
The new school : how the information age will save American education from itself / Glenn Harlan Reynolds.
pages   cm
Includes bibliographical references and index.
ISBN 978-1-59403-710-8 (hardcover : alk. paper)
ISBN 978-1-59403-711-5 (ebook) 1. Public schools—United States.
2. Educational change—United States.
3. Education—Effect of technological innovations on. I. Title.
LA217.2.R495 2014
370.973—dc23
2013033387

CONTENTS

PREFACE AND ACKNOWLEDGMENTS

I never meant to write about education. Though I've spent most of my life in the educational world, as a teacher or a student, writing *about* education never really crossed my mind.

That changed when I wrote a few columns and a short law-review article starting back in 2009. It's said that academics never question the model for their own industry until they have to send their own kids to school, and there's something to that. It's also the case that education, over the past few years, has become considerably more interesting – not just to me but also to others. Aviation became more interesting after the Wright brothers, space travel became more interesting after von Braun, and computers became more interesting after Steve Jobs. When the system of the world is changing, there's more to talk about.

That's happening now. I began tracing this change in columns written for the *Washington Examiner, USA Today,* and the *New York Post,* then expanded it into two short Broadsides for Encounter Books: *The Higher Education Bubble* and *The K-12 Implosion.* Pleased by the reception that those got, publisher Roger Kimball asked me to tie those two treatments together and to expand them into a full-length book. That's what I've attempted here. Even expanded, this is more of a conversation starter than a conversation ender. I make no claims about knowing what is coming next in any great detail; the best I can do is echo Webb Wilder: I can't predict the future, but I can take a hint. Fortunately, this is an area where hints abound.

Along the way, I've had very interesting conversations with too many people to mention: I am not the only one who finds this subject of increasing importance. But in particular, I've had valuable discussions with my colleague Ben Barton, whose work overlaps with mine; with my father, Charles Reynolds, whose thoughts on the future of higher education I found particularly interesting; and with my brother Jonathan Reynolds, who has looked at these issues from a different, but complementary, perspective. I also spent some time at Stanford's Hoover Institution, a leader in research on K-12 reform, where I spoke with numerous experts and took advantage of their generously provided resources.

In working on this project, I've enjoyed excellent research assistance along the way from Jesse Ford, John Higgins, Leigh Outten, and Jessica Molinaro. (Some of them didn't know that they were helping me with this particular project, because at the time I hadn't figured that out yet.) And, of course, I appreciate the support and encouragement of my dean, Doug Blaze, and the University of Tennessee College of Law, which has always supported and encouraged my research interests, however unconventional.

One final prefatory note: As will become clear, when the subtitle of this book talks about technology saving American education from itself, I don't mean simply online schooling or the dumb but popular "Let's give every kid an iPad" approach to educational technology. Technology matters because it provides more options, not simply because of bells and whistles. Indeed, some of the most important technologies described here are really social technologies, like homeschooling and "flipped" classrooms. Our education problems will not be solved by gadgets alone but by changed methods that are, in some cases, made possible by gadgets.

In the Beginning

FROM THE 1ST CENTURY AND BEFORE TO THE 21ST

It all started a long time ago. Although today's schools – both K-12 and universities – spend a lot of time talking about the future, their models are based on the past. To be exact, American education at both levels is largely based on models imported from Germany in the 19th century, models that served 19th century purposes well but that may be poorly adapted to the needs of the 21st. It is becoming steadily more obvious that those models are beginning to fail and that we will need new models for the future.

At one time, of course, those 19th century models seemed modern themselves. And, in fact, they represented huge progress in their day. But they represented a major departure from the previous entirety of human history, and it may be that the industrial model they represented was a temporary detour. For most of human history, after all, education wasn't a product but a process, a part of everyday living.

LIFE AMONG THE SAVAGES

From the caveman era to classical times, formal education was largely unknown. Children weren't sent off to school but instead spent their time around adults, watching them go about the business of the day, being pressed into service as helpers, and learning by osmosis or through one-on-one instruction. The most dangerous activities – say, hunting mammoths – were adult-only, but kids grew up quickly and were soon part of the adult world. That modern creature, the teenager, did not exist: people in their teens were mostly adults.

A few specialists – shamans or flint-knappers – might have had apprentices, but the instruction was still one on one and hands-on. There weren't books, because there wasn't writing yet. There weren't schools, because there weren't subjects to be taught that favored lecturers standing in front of groups of students all learning the same thing.

Over time, with the invention of writing and with the growth of kingdoms, empires, and – perhaps most significant – organized religion, on-the-job training ceased to be the only way to learn. Written language meant that some people (though a minority, usually) needed to know how to read and write, something better taught in sit-down sessions. Wealthy families (and sometimes middle-class families) hired tutors to impart at least the basics of literacy, arithmetic, and culture. Later, eminent scholars would gather pupils around for advanced lessons in philosophy and other subjects, forming the seeds of what would later become higher education.

But even as late as the 18th century, most people had little or no formal classroom education; even the rich often learned their letters at home, and although there were colleges and universities throughout the Western world, they were largely finishing schools for the elites and training centers for ecclesiastics. In the rest of the world, education was still an informal process.[1]

STANDARDIZED PARTS AND MASS PRODUCTION

Thus, for thousands of years, education was more or less the same. Then came the Industrial Revolution, and suddenly, the old way didn't work well enough. Society needed educated workers in vastly greater numbers, and it needed them to be educated in particular ways. It was time for something different, for education based on an industrial model.

The Industrial Revolution was marked by two things: specialization and economies of scale. With these two came a third: standardization. The result was a vast increase in productive capacity, making people richer and healthier. A *lot* richer and healthier. In his book, *The Escape from Hunger and Premature Death, 1700–2100,*[2] historian Robert Fogel notes that the improvement in living conditions for the working classes in industrial countries during the Industrial Revolution is without any parallel in human history. Life expectancies got much longer (from 32 in 1725 to 76 in 1990 in the U.K.);[3] people grew taller and were sick less often, with much better nutrition. The poor of today are much better off in most ways than the aristocrats of the pre-industrial era. But there were costs.

Along with increased health and wealth, industrialization created a lot of social strain as traditional ways of living were disrupted by new ways of doing business. William Blake's "Dark Satanic mills" weren't as bad as they're remembered today – if they had been, people wouldn't have flocked to them. Or maybe it's fairer to say that, bad as they were, they were still better than life as a subsistence farmer, where backbreaking labor got you all you could eat in a good year, but where the same backbreaking labor could leave you starving in a bad one anyway. But this new industrial world was very different from life on the farm.

Prior to the Industrial Revolution, most skills were hands-on skills, or at least skills readily learned one on one. In a small-scale workplace, there was more flexibility about how things got done. Blacksmiths often had their own individual techniques, and it didn't matter much because blacksmithing was pretty much a one-man job, with perhaps some help from an apprentice or two. (It's not easy, either: in high school, I took an interest in it, and with a couple of friends we put together suits of Roman armor – a *lorica segmentata* each – that we hand-riveted and assembled. I then read some books on what was involved in *real* blacksmithing and quailed.) A blacksmith who was out late the night before could start a bit later the next morning, or skip lunch, or take a day off to go fishing, or just spend extra time on a piece if he thought it was worthwhile.

If you wanted a hundred times more blacksmithing output than a single blacksmith could produce, you had to get 99 more blacksmiths to do it. And each of them would still be working more or less on his own. With no division of labor or mass production, there was no economy of scale.

This single-laborer practice changed with the Industrial Revolution, as clearly explained by Adam Smith in his famous description of a pin factory from *The Wealth of Nations:*

> *A workman not educated to this business ... could scarce, perhaps, with his utmost industry, make one pin in one day, and certainly could not make twenty. But in the way in which this business is now carried on, not only the whole work is a peculiar trade, but it is divided into a number of branches, of which the greater part are likewise peculiar trades. One man draws out the wire; another straights it; a third cuts it; a fourth points it; a fifth grinds it at the top for receiving the head; to make the head requires two or three distinct operations; to put it on is a peculiar business, to whiten the pins is another; it is even a trade by itself to put them into the paper.... Those ten persons, therefore, could make among them upwards of forty-eight thousand pins in a day.... But if they had all wrought separately and independently, and without any of them having been educated to this peculiar business, they certainly could not each of them have made twenty, perhaps not one pin in a day; that is, certainly, not the two hundred and fortieth, perhaps not the four thousand eight hundredth part of what they are at present capable of performing, in consequence of a proper division and combination of their different operations.*[4]

Division of labor allowed large groups to be organized in ways that were actually *more* efficient than smaller groups or collections of individuals acting independently. Big machinery allowed big jobs to be done, but because the machinery itself was big, it could *only* do big jobs efficiently. When the smallest efficient steam engine is big enough to power a whole factory, it doesn't make sense to use it for anything less: the cost is the same, but the return is smaller. Thus the "minimum efficient scale" turns out to be pretty big. And lots of capital and lots of time and energy are required to fuel these big operations.

So no more blacksmiths under spreading chestnut trees. The price for the efficiency gains in Smith's pin factory was that the workers couldn't operate "separately and independently." Each had to do his assigned piece of the operation predictably, consistently, and in coordination with the others. Big factories full of workers had to operate the same way: when it takes a huge steam engine to power the factory, everyone needs to be at his (or her) machine when the steam engine starts up, and they need to stay there consistently until it shuts down again. Otherwise, its output is wasted.

With jobs broken up into various small, repetitive tasks, as Smith describes, workers have to be patient (because it's boring), reliable (because one task depends on another), and good at following instructions (because the tasks often don't make obvious intuitive sense). And while factory work wasn't rocket science, it required kinds of knowledge – basic literacy, arithmetic, and measuring skills – that subsistence farming and other basic trades did not.

Some of these skills – measuring, for example – could be taught on the shop floor. But reading and writing and arithmetic, even at crude levels, were hard to teach among the whirring machines. And the even more important skills of punctuality, orderliness, and precise attention to directions were harder still.

Military organizations had been teaching these kinds of skills for a while, and so it's perhaps not surprising that the educational approach aimed at teaching them to future workers came from those devotees of martial orderliness, the Prussians. It was an approach that was explicitly aimed at producing punctual, obedient factory workers; orderly citizens; and loyal soldiers.

In 19th century America, the Prussians had a good reputation. Americans traveled to Europe to look at their schools, and they brought back a system of education modeled on 19th century Germany. This was despite the fact that U.S. literacy rates were already extremely high under the decentralized education system then in existence:

> *Haphazard and locally controlled as this educational "system" was, Americans were amazingly literate. Newspapers were the major forum for communication during the Revolutionary period. With dizzying speed, they mobilized the nation against the Stamp Act, the Navigation Acts, and actions taken by the royally appointed colonial governors. During the Revolutionary War, Thomas Paine's Common Sense sold 100,000 copies, and it is thought that 25 percent of the white adult population read the book. A study of a Vermont county at the time of the American Revolution found "almost universal male signature literacy," with the rate of female literacy ranging from "60 percent to 90 percent," depending on the locality's level of commercial development.*[5]

Nonetheless, American thought leaders looked to the Germans for a model of public education that better suited their sensibilities. One of the most enthusiastic and influential of these Americans was public education pioneer Horace Mann, then serving as the secretary of Massachusetts' Board of Education. Mann admired the Prussian system:

> *Upon assuming his new responsibilities, Mann traveled to several European countries to inspect their school systems. Ignoring the locally controlled Scottish and English*

systems that had been the model for colonial schools, he made careful note of the skill with which the Prussians were using public schools to unify the German people. Centralized institutions, a state-directed curriculum, statistical information, and professional cadres were being mobilized to create a unified national spirit, a common language, and an identity that would transcend parochial loyalties.[6]

On his return, Mann extolled the Prussian model in his seventh annual report. This met with some resistance, as critics accused him of wanting to establish a "Prussian-style tyranny" in the schools, arguing that the Prussian model was based on a presumption that the government was wiser than the citizenry, while in America the presumption was the reverse. There was considerable basis for this complaint. Prussian theorists regarded public education, and higher education as well, as an institution of "police" and a way of making students "useful as future tools,"[7] – but Mann's idea ultimately caught on for the most part. Mann wanted to remake society, and he wanted to start with children. In his turn of phrase, "men are cast-iron, but children are wax."[8] Just as the Prussian model had as much to do with political and social ordering as with teaching and learning, so it was with Mann's Americanized Prussian model.

This approach not only reflected Mann's social views but also met the economic needs of the day. Thus, the traditional public school: like a factory, it runs by the bell. Like machines in a factory, desks and students are lined up in orderly rows. When shifts (classes) change, the bell rings again, and students go on to the next class. And within each class, the subjects are the same, the assignments are the same, and the examinations are the same, regardless of the characteristics of individual students.

This was quite a change from the traditional public school's predecessor, the one-room schoolhouse, where students of different ages were mixed together and where assignments often varied even among students of the same age. A teacher in a one-room schoolhouse was like a blacksmith, doing the whole job in his or her own way. A teacher in a modern industrial-era school was like a factory worker, performing standardized operations on standardized parts. And the standardized parts – the students – were taught along the way how to fit into a larger machine.

Like the difference between artisanal blacksmithing and industrial metalwork, the modern school system provided far less scope for individuality on the part of both its producers and its products. But the trade-off was seen as worthwhile: the modern assembly-line approach, in both settings, produced more of what society wanted, and it did so at a lower cost. If standard parts are what you want, an assembly line is better than a blacksmith. (Interestingly, Horace Mann's children were homeschooled.)[9]

Of course, the industrial approach had both upsides and downsides, and over time the ills of the industrial model also set in. Just as an assembly-line worker, in performing the same repetitive task over and over again, loses touch with the end product – and tends to focus on job descriptions over substance – so too did industrial-model teachers lose touch with the ultimate goal of producing an educated person. And with public employees, most notably teachers, becoming de facto or de jure unionized, public school systems began to suffer from the same kinds of labor and productivity problems that plagued industrial-era manufacturing concerns by the late 20th century – bloated pensions, reduced productivity, and the inability to fire incompetent employees. Quality suffered as a result. But despite wave after wave of "reform" efforts – all of which typically had the effect of putting more power into the hands of central offices and education professionals, at the expense of parents and localities – by the turn of the millennium, there was widespread sentiment that the traditional Mann model wasn't working. The question, then, was what would come next.

*   *   *

FROM FINISHING SCHOOL TO PROFESSORS' (AND ADMINISTRATORS') PARADISE

In the higher education field, meanwhile, German ideas were also taking hold, though their implementation looked much different. Until the second half of the 19th century, American universities followed a traditional English model, being largely places for the education of preachers and the polishing of wealthy scions, with room for a few scholarly types as well. The model was not a notable success, and college enrollment actually shrank from 1850 to 1870. As Brown University's president, Francis Wayland, remarked, "We have produced an article for which the demand is diminishing."[10] But after the Civil War, American higher education changed.

On the one hand, the Morrill Act – passed while the Civil War was still raging – provided land grants for schools that provided useful education (originally focusing on engineering, agriculture, and military science) to the masses. Further, the demands of the industrial model of K-12 education led to a need for teachers, which was met by the appearance of so-called Normal Schools – teachers' colleges – that focused on such training.

On the other hand, American higher education was also very impressed with its German counterparts. (In addition, no doubt, American academics were impressed with the fact that the professoriate in Germany enjoyed considerably more prestige than did the professoriate in America.)[11] The German model of a research university – focused on graduate education, original research, and scholarly education rather than on lecturing to undergraduates – appealed to many.

German universities stressed academic freedom and featured an innovation called the seminar, in which students and faculty interacted. This was a considerable departure from traditional lecture classes. American students visited German universities and returned home speaking highly of their experiences; American academics visited and found much to emulate.

By 1871, the first seminar in America was offered by Charles Kendall Adams at the University of Michigan, but this was soon copied widely.[12] In 1876, Johns Hopkins University was founded in an explicit effort to import Germanic styles of higher education, and other schools on a similar model – Cornell, Stanford, the University of Chicago, Clark University (future home of Robert Goddard) – soon appeared.[13]

The German research-university model quickly caught on, and schools that initially resisted the change – like Yale and Princeton – soon realized that they'd have to go along or be left behind. In the academic world, scholarly research and the production of graduate students who would, in time, go on to teach at other institutions became the standard for success. Teaching undergraduates, the traditional role of colleges, was less significant. Colleges that focused on undergraduate teaching remained, but as colleges, they were seen as less prestigious than universities.

German-influenced Johns Hopkins set the tone, and its graduates carried the torch:

The foremost objective of Johns Hopkins was ... to provide advanced instruction of a standard comparable to that being set in Germany. ... Until 1890, graduate students outnumbered undergraduates by a wide margin, and the majority of Hopkins A.B.'s actually remained at the school for some graduate work. Hopkins consequently gave an impetus to American graduate education and did much to standardize the American Ph.D. at a credibly high level. Hopkins produced more Ph.D.'s during the 1870s and 1880s than Harvard and Yale combined. By the 1890s these made-in-America scholars were carrying the Hopkins spirit into all the major universities of the country. Graduate education entails research, however, and Hopkins far more than any other contemporary American university actively encouraged original investigations by its faculty. Here, too, the con-

tribution of the university was something more than the sum of the works of its distinguished faculty. The scholars at Hopkins aggressively seized vanguard positions in their respective disciplines, particularly through the organization of scholarly journals. Five of the six original departments sponsored such journals, several of which became the central organ of their discipline. Other periodicals followed, wholly or partly lodged at the university. These publications in turn played an indispensable role in the emergence of academic disciplines. Perhaps most important, Johns Hopkins enlarged the range of possibilities in American higher education and by doing so also enlarged the consciousness of educators to include a concrete university research role.[14]

Thus, by the turn of the 20th century, the model was set. The highest academic exemplar was the research university, producing published research and sending its graduates out to serve as faculty at other (even if lesser) institutions. And, of course, in this model the prolific professor with a stable of graduate students under his tutelage reigned supreme.

Indeed, the establishment of Hopkins, Chicago, Stanford, et al., produced something new in American academia: *Moneyball*-style competition for faculty. As University of Michigan President James Angell commented in 1892, "Whereas formerly it was rather rare that a professor was called from one institution to another, now the custom is very general."[15] By *called*, of course, he meant *enticed*, usually with promises of salary increases and, even more important, support for research. When the University of Chicago opened, it lured away 15 top professors from Clark University alone, a blow from which Clark never fully recovered.[16] As always happens in such competitive environments, this threat also pressured schools to preemptively spend more on existing faculty stars, lest they be "called" to another institution.

With this star system showing rewards not only in money but also in the real coin of the academic realm, prestige,[17] even the land-grant schools and teachers' colleges got into the act, over time pushing graduate education at the expense of undergraduate teaching and doing what they could to move up the prestige ladder: plenty of institutions that style themselves as universities today started out as teachers' colleges.

This trend toward academic upward mobility accelerated when government money entered the picture in a big way. For a while, tendencies to de-emphasize undergraduate education were somewhat restrained by institutions' need to bring in enough tuition money to keep the lights on. The boom in college enrollment helped, but the problem with financing research via tuition dollars is that the more students you bring in, the more students you have to teach – and teaching isn't research. With federal research grants, which became widely available after World War II, tuition revenue wasn't as important. And with federal student aid exploding in the last quarter of the 20th century, undergraduates became less sensitive about costs, which also helped universities pad their bottom lines.

Higher education in the late 20th century gradually became something of a bubble, in which prices – tuition – rose faster than their likely return in the form of graduates' wages, something that has really come to a head since the onset of harder economic times. Indeed, talk of a "higher education bubble" has become common as unemployed graduates wonder how they will pay back massive student loans and as parents and prospective students begin to view the value of a college degree with increased skepticism.

All good things come to an end. The 19th century models of both "higher" and "lower" education were useful in their day, but this is no longer the 19th century. In the pages that follow, we will look at how we got into our current predicament, and at how we will, in the coming decades, get out of it.

Higher Education

THE BURSTING BUBBLE

THE PROBLEM IN A NUTSHELL

If something cannot go on forever, it will stop.
ECONOMIST HERBERT STEIN

In other words, something that can't go on forever, won't. It's a story of an industry that may sound familiar.

The buyers think what they're buying will appreciate in value, making them rich in the future. The product grows more and more elaborate, and more and more expensive, but the expense is offset by cheap credit provided by sellers eager to encourage buyers to buy.

Buyers see that everyone else is taking on mounds of debt, and so they are more comfortable when they do so themselves; besides, for a generation, the value of what they're buying has gone up steadily. What could go wrong? Everything continues smoothly until, at some point, it doesn't anymore.

Yes, this sounds like the housing bubble, but I'm afraid it's also sounding a lot like a still-inflating higher education bubble. And despite (or because of) the fact that my day job involves higher education, I think it's better for us to face up to what's going on *before* the bubble bursts too messily. Because that's what's likely to happen.

No one disputes that college has gotten a lot more expensive. A recent *Money* magazine report notes, "After adjusting for financial aid, the amount families pay for college has sky-rocketed 439% since 1982.... Normal supply and demand can't begin to explain cost increases of this magnitude."[1]

Consumers would balk, except for two things.

First – as with the housing bubble – cheap and readily available credit has let people borrow to finance education. They're willing to do so because of (1) consumer ignorance, as students (and, often, their parents) don't fully grasp just how harsh the impact of student-loan payments will be after graduation; and (2) a belief that, whatever the cost, a college education is a necessary ticket to future prosperity. Second, there's a belief that college is an essential entry ticket to the middle class, regardless of whatever actual value it might provide.

Bubbles form when too many people expect values to go up forever. Bubbles burst when there are no longer enough excessively optimistic and ignorant folks to fuel them. And there are signs that this is beginning to happen already where education is concerned.

A 2010 *New York Times* profile described Cortney Munna, then a 26-year-old graduate of New York University with nearly $100,000 in student-loan debt – debt that her degree in religious and women's studies did not equip her to repay. Payments on the debt are about $700 per month, equivalent to a respectable house payment, and a major bite on her monthly income of $2,300 as a photographer's assistant earning an hourly wage.

And, unlike a bad mortgage on an underwater house, Munna can't simply walk away from her student loans, which cannot be expunged in a bankruptcy. She's stuck in a financial trap.

Some might say that she deserves it. Who borrows $100,000 to finance a degree in religious and women's studies that won't make you any money? She should have wised up, and others should learn from her mistake instead of learning too late as she did: "I don't want to spend the rest of my life slaving away to pay for an education I got for four years and would happily give back."[2] But Munna is not the only one. Many recent grads are in the same boat.

Another appalling *New York Times* profile demonstrated even worse problems in the graduate school world, telling the story of veterinarian Hayley Schafer, who graduated from veterinary school with over $312,000 in student-loan debt. Veterinary practice had been her "dream job" since the age of 5, and she made it, but at a price. Nor is she alone:

They don't teach much at veterinary school about bears, particularly the figurative kind, although debt as large and scary as any grizzly shadows most vet school grads, usually for decades. Nor is there much in the curriculum about the prospects for graduates or the current state of the profession. Neither, say many professors and doctors, looks very promising. The problem is a boom in supply (that is, vets) and a decline in demand (namely, veterinary services). Class sizes have been rising at nearly every school, in some cases by as much as 20 percent in recent years. And the cost of vet school has far outpaced the rate of inflation. It has risen to a median of $63,000 a year for out-of-state tuition, fees and living expenses, according to the Association of American Veterinary Medical Colleges, up 35 percent in the last decade.

This would seem less alarming if vets made more money. But starting salaries have sunk by about 13 percent during the same 10-year period, in inflation-adjusted terms, to $45,575 a year, according to the American Veterinary Medical Association.[3]

Unfortunately, a lot of students, in a lot of fields, are facing a similar problem to greater or lesser degrees. Concern over high student-loan debt and poor job prospects was a major theme in the Occupy protests as well:

When graduation day passes without a decent job offer, frustration builds. It continues building as recent grads move back in with their parents, work unpaid internships, settle for a job they might have gotten without a degree – and continue to pay their student loan bills each month.

That frustration is often at the heart of Occupy Wall Street protests in New York's financial districts and cities across the country. Although the leaderless revolution does not have any stated objectives, many participants are calling for student loan forgiveness. . . . Student loans are mentioned over and over in handwritten stories posted on the Tumblr account "We are the 99 Percent." One student wrote: "When I graduate I will have (over) $100K in student loans, as will much of my generation." Another wrote: "I am a freshman in college with 12K+ in student loan debts ALREADY." A man wrote: "I am 42 years old . . . I owe $40,000 in student loans."[4]

In discussing the Occupy demonstrations, Professor Kenneth Anderson notes the role of declining returns on education and the struggles between the upper and lower tiers of the "New Class," the educated managerial elite that has dominated U.S. society since World War II:

The upper tier is still doing pretty well. But the lower tier of the New Class – the machine by which universities trained young people to become minor regulators and then delivered them into white collar positions on the basis of credentials in history, political science, literature, ethnic and women's studies – with or without the benefit of law school – has broken down. The supply is uninterrupted, but the demand has dried up. The agony of the students getting dumped at the far end of the supply chain is in large part the OWS. As Above the Law points out, here is "John," who got out of undergrad, spent a year unemployed and living at home, and is now apparently at University of Vermont law school, with its top ranked environmental law program – John wants to work at a "nonprofit."

Even more frightening is the young woman who grad-

uated from UC Berkeley, wanting to work in "sustainable conservation." She is now raising chickens at home, dying wool and knitting knick-knacks to sell at craft fairs. Her husband has been studying criminal justice and EMT – i.e., preparing to work for government in some of California's hitherto most lucrative positions – but as those work possibilities have dried up, he is hedging with a (sensible) apprenticeship as an electrician. These young people are looking at serious downward mobility, in income as well as status. The prospects of the lower tier New Class semi-professionals are dissolving at an alarming rate. Student-loan debt is a large part of its problems, but that's essentially a cost question accompanying a loss of demand for these professionals' services.

The OWS protestors are a revolt – a shrill, cri-de-cœur wail at the betrayal of class solidarity – of the lower tier New Class against the upper tier New Class. It was, after all, the upper tier New Class, the private-public finance consortium, that created the student loan business and inflated the bubble in which these lower tier would-be professionals borrowed the money. It's a securitization machine, not so very different from the subprime mortgage machine. The asset bubble pops, but the upper tier New Class, having insulated itself and, as with subprime, having taken its cut up front and passed the risk along, is still doing pretty well. It's not populism versus the bankers so much as internecine warfare between two tiers of elites.

The downward mobility is real, however, in both income and status. The Cal graduate started out wanting to do "sustainable conservation." She is now engaged in something closer to subsistence farming.[5]

New Class politics aside, the problem is straightforward: tuition costs have grown to a point at which future income often isn't enough to pay off the debt – when there's a job available at all. When this phenomenon affects bartenders or beauticians, it generates a distant sympathy, but when it affects people of the same general social class as, say, most media folks, it gets more attention. The phenomenon – and the risk of downward mobility, made worse by the millstone weight of student-loan debt – is indeed real, and not limited to members of the "helping professions" and public/private bureaucracy.

But bubbles burst when people catch on, and there's some evidence that people are beginning to catch on. Student-loan debt, once regarded by many as "good debt," is now seen as toxic – as any consumer of financial-advice shows like Suze Orman, Dave Ramsey, or Clark Howard can attest – and students are expressing a willingness to go to a cheaper school rather than run up debt. Things haven't collapsed yet, but they're looking shakier – kind of like the housing market looked in 2007.

So what happens if the bubble collapses? Will it be a tragedy, with millions of Americans losing their path to higher-paying jobs? Maybe not. College is often described as a path to prosperity, but is it? A college education can help people make more money in three ways.

First, it may actually make them more economically productive by teaching them skills valued in the workplace: computer programming, nursing, or engineering, say. (Religious and women's studies, not so much.)

Second, it may provide a credential that employers want – not because it represents actual skills but because it's a weeding tool that doesn't produce civil-rights suits as, say, IQ tests might. A four-year college degree, even if its holder acquired no actual skills, at least indicates some ability to show up on time and perform as instructed. These traits, essential in the industrial economy, remain pretty important even in our post-industrial era.

Third, a college degree – at least an elite one – may hook its holder up with a useful social network that can provide jobs and opportunities in the future. (This is perhaps truer if it's a degree from Yale than if it's one from Eastern Kentucky – unless you're planning on living in eastern Kentucky after graduation – but it's true everywhere to some degree.)

While an individual might rationally pursue all three of these, only the first one – actual added skills – produces a net benefit for society. The other two are just distributional; they're about who gets the goodies, not about making more of them.

Yet today's college education system seems to be in the business of selling parts 2 and 3 to a much greater degree than part 1, along with selling the even-harder-to-quantify "college experience," which as often as not boils down to four (or more) years of partying.

Post-bubble, perhaps students – and employers, not to mention parents and lenders – will focus instead on education that fosters economic value. And that is likely to press colleges to focus more on providing useful majors. (That doesn't necessarily rule out traditional liberal-arts majors, as long as they are rigorous and require a real general education, rather than trendy and easy subjects, but the key word here is *rigorous*.)

My question is whether traditional academic institutions will be able to keep up with the times, or whether – as Anya Kamenetz suggests in her book, *DIY U* – the real pioneering will be in online education and the work of "edupunks" who are more interested in finding new ways of teaching and learning than in protecting existing interests.

I'm betting on the latter. Industries seldom reform themselves, and real competition usually comes from the outside. But if we're lucky, I'll be wrong about that, and the higher education sector will play a big role in its own reinvention.

In this section, we'll look briefly at how the higher education bubble came to be, the problems it is creating, and what is likely to happen when – and after – the bursting takes place. We'll also look at a few things readers can do for themselves and for the country.

*   *   *

HOW WE GOT HERE

Higher education has been around for a long time. The University of Bologna was started in 1088, and many other European universities date from the 12th, 13th, and 14th centuries. It has been a presence in the United States from the very earliest days of colonization – long enough ago that Harvard University supposedly once offered Galileo a job. But for most of that time, a college education, to say nothing of graduate study, was a luxury: colleges and universities catered mostly to the rich, and to the clergy, with the occasional deserving scholarship student thrown in.

College was not seen as the primary way for a young man – it was pretty much always a young man back then – to get ahead, at least not unless the young man was planning a career as a man of the cloth. Most lawyers, and even most doctors, learned more through apprenticeship and on-the-job training than through formal education, which is not surprising, since that was the way most people learned what they needed to know for their jobs.

Instead, a college education was mostly a way for a young man of distinction to obtain a degree of social polish – and wider social connections – while sowing a few discreet (or, sometimes, not so discreet) wild oats. College was not sold as an economic investment in the future but rather as a stage in life, and no one was handing out loans to aspiring entrants.

This began to change after the Civil War, and the reason was, naturally enough, federal money. Even before the Civil War, reformer Justin Morrill had been talking up the idea of colleges and universities dedicated to training farmers, mechanics, and soldiers rather than clergymen and lawyers. Morrill's original scheme involved colleges modeled on West Point, with free tuition and admission via congressional nomination. This proposal went through several different versions, one of which was vetoed by President James Buchanan on the eve of the Civil War, but a later bill was signed into law by Abraham Lincoln.

As it was finally passed, the Morrill Act offered land grants to institutions that would offer education in farming and mechanics, along with a spot of military training. Though the traditional colleges looked down on these upstarts as little better than trade schools, many became elite universities, ranging from Virginia Tech, Texas A&M, and the University of Tennessee to the University of Wisconsin, MIT, and Cornell. Historians now regard the Morrill Act as a major step forward in education and a major booster for the U.S. economy, and many believe that the (then required) military training played a major role in America's success in World Wars I and II.

Well, if some is good, more must be better. That was the thinking after World War II, when policymakers, wondering how to receive a flood of returning GIs, hit upon the idea of sending them to college. The GI Bill gave millions of discharged soldiers the option of going to school instead of hitting the job market all at once, which many feared would lead to a return of Depression-era unemployment. Many took advantage of it, and colleges and universities, anxious to accommodate them (and to share in the federal largesse), embarked upon ambitious programs of expansion.

By the time the flood of veterans from World War II and Korea was slowing to a trickle, the baby boomers were beginning to show up, and the Vietnam War soon added yet another reason for college: student draft deferments. Enrollments swelled again, and colleges expanded further. By the 1970s, the infrastructure was there for more college students than the population was ready to produce on its own. The solution? Expanded federal aid in the form of Pell Grants, guaranteed student loans, and other support. This really took off in the mid- to late 1970s.

The result was predictable. As with any subsidized product, prices rose to absorb the subsidy. And as colleges saw that increases in tuition didn't hurt enrollment – higher tuition often made a school seem more prestigious, and anyway there were cheap government loans to make up the difference –

the rate of increase climbed even further. How much further? Just look at this graphic from University of Michigan economics and finance Professor Mark Perry at the Carpe Diem economics blog.

COLLEGE TUITION VS. MEDICAL CARE VS. HOME PRICES VS. CPI

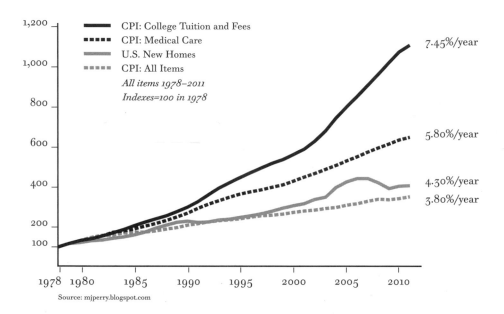

Source: mjperry.blogspot.com

As you can see, at an annual growth rate of 7.45 percent a year, tuition has vastly outstripped the consumer price index (CPI) and health care prices, while the growth in house prices under the housing bubble looks like a mere bump in the road by comparison. For a while, parents could look to increased home values to make them feel better about paying Junior's tuition (the so-called wealth effect, in which increases in asset values make people more comfortable about spending), or they could at least borrow against the equity in their homes to fund tuition. But that equity is gone now, and tuition is still climbing.

So where does that leave us? Even students who major in programs shown to increase earnings, like engineering, face limits to how much debt they can sanely amass. With costs approaching $60,000 a year for many private schools and out-of-state costs at many state schools exceeding $40,000 (and often closing in on $30,000 for in-state students), some people are graduating with debts of $100,000 or more – sometimes much more.

That's dangerous even if you get a job as an engineer. (Engineers get laid off too.) It's absurdly dangerous if you're in a field that doesn't produce higher earnings. And the problem is not a small one. According to Professor Richard Vedder, writing in the *Chronicle of Higher Education*, the number of student-loan debtors actually equals the number of people with college degrees. (How is this possible? "First, huge numbers of those borrowing money *never* graduate from college. Second, many who borrow are not in baccalaureate degree programs. Three, people take forever to pay their loans back."[6]) Total student-loan debt in America has passed the trillion-dollar mark:[7] more than total credit-card debt and more than total auto-loan debt. Investors, meanwhile, are spurning student-loan-related investments in light of rising default rates, suggesting that they also view the situation as unsustainable.[8] JPMorgan Chase, the largest student-loan lender, is exiting the field in what some see as a parallel move to its exit from subprime lending in 2007.[9]

The rule of thumb is that college-debt payments should account for less than 8 percent of gross income. Otherwise, watch out – and remember that loan payments are usually not dischargeable in bankruptcy. The loans can follow you for decades. Students graduating with heavy burdens of student-loan debt must choose (if they can) jobs that pay enough money to cover the payments, often limiting their career choices to an extent they didn't foresee in their student days. And even students who can earn enough to service their debts may find themselves constrained in other ways: it's hard to get a mortgage, for example, when you're already, in effect, paying one in the form of student loans.

This has implications for the housing bubble, too, of course, since the traditional source of new home buyers and move-up home buyers – people a few years out of college or grad school – now suffers from an unprecedented debt burden. And, in fact, there's considerable evidence that student-loan debt is already slowing the economy, as indebted students put off marriage, new cars, or house purchases because they're already hurting financially. A *New York Times* article profiled several graduates in just such a fix. For example:

> *Consider Shane Gill, a 33-year-old high-school teacher in New York City. He does not have a car. He does not own a home. He is not married. And he is no anomaly: like hundreds of thousands of others in his generation, he has put off such major purchases or decisions in part because of his debts.*
>
> *Mr. Gill owes about $45,000 in federal student loans, plus another $40,000 to his parents. That investment in his future has led to a secure job with decent pay and good benefits. But it has left him with tremendous financial constraints, as he faces chipping away at the debt for years on end.*
>
> *"There's this anxiety: what if I decided I wanted to get married or have children?" Mr. Gill said. "I don't know how I would. And that adds to the sense of precariousness. There's a persistent, buzzing kind of toothache around it."*[10]

A study by the Federal Reserve Bank of New York underscores the problem:

> [T]*he share of twenty-five-year-olds with student debt has increased from just 25 percent in 2003 to 43 percent in 2012.... Student loan delinquencies have also been growing.*[11]

The Federal Reserve also found that those with student-loan debt were substantially less likely to purchase houses or cars than those without student loans. This isn't surprising. That "persistent, buzzing kind of toothache" sensation doesn't encourage people to live large. But with young people traditionally being a major source of demand in both the housing and auto markets, two areas deemed important to economic recovery and prosperity – buying first houses and first cars and then moving up to something fancier every few years – this burden is sure to be a drag on the economy as a whole.

And that's for graduates who have jobs. It's even worse, of course, when graduates *can't* find jobs that will let them cover the payments. Regardless of the student's employment circumstances, the debt still comes due. Students can enter forbearance, but that only reduces or stops the payments for a while; the principal continues to grow. Only death or (sometimes) disability will get rid of the debt, and for private student loans, co-signers may remain liable even if the borrower dies. The whole scheme, as several commentators have noted, seems like the debt-slavery regimes used by coal mines and plantations to keep workers and sharecroppers in debt peonage for life. (Some newer graduates may be eligible for "income-based repayment" schemes, which make things somewhat better, but not that much.)

For some of these unfortunates, the debt is enough to quash marriage plans (who wants to marry someone with huge amounts of unpayable debt?), prevent homeownership, and generally wreak havoc on the debtors' lives. These people may wind up living in their parents' basements until they are old enough to collect Social Security, which may wind up being garnisheed – no joke – for unpaid student debts.

It's a big problem, and more and more students and potential students are becoming aware of just how bad student debt can be. That's causing them to change their behavior. Some are eschewing college entirely in favor of military service, skilled trades, or lower-cost alternatives like community college. Others are skipping expensive private colleges (especially those outside the top tier) in favor of less expensive state schools. Some are pursuing their educations online. And even those still going to traditional colleges or universities are looking more closely at their majors and the employment prospects after graduation. Nor are graduate programs immune: the number of students taking the Law School Admissions Test, for example, has fallen by 25 percent each year over the past two years, leading some to predict that lower-tier law schools may be entering a "death spiral."[12]

These are all rational responses to the fact that the traditional approach to higher education no longer makes as much sense. When education was cheap enough that students could pay their own way through by working part-time, "study what interests you" was reasonable advice. Some criticize today's students for being more concerned about return on investment than about pure learning, but when the investment runs well into the six figures, students would be crazy *not* to worry about the return it generates. The difference between an investment and a consumption item is that an investment can be expected to pay for itself eventually. A consumption item just involves the exchange of cash for something that is, well, consumed. A six-figure consumption item is well beyond the resources of college students – nobody would advise an 18-year-old to purchase a Ferrari on borrowed money, after all – but if a college education is a consumption item, not an investment, then that's basically what they are doing.

But as the behavior that led to the bubble changes, the bubble itself will burst, and things in the higher education world will never be quite the same. That has significant ramifications for both students and faculties. The next section looks at some of those.

WHAT HAPPENS WHEN THE BUBBLE BURSTS?

For the past several decades, higher education has been living high on the hog. Faculty salaries have grown significantly, and administrative salaries have grown dramatically: seven-figure pay for university presidents isn't even news anymore, and, at most schools, there are scores of lower-level officials who still make more money than anyone else on campus except coaches. (In every state, the highest paid state employee is in higher education, though there are more coaches on the list than university presidents.)[13] Institutions of higher learning have been on a building boom, running up new administration buildings, athletic facilities, dormitories, recreation centers, and classrooms.

All of this is predicated on the money's continuing to roll in. But what if it stops? Already, state and local aid to higher education is shrinking[14] as states face pension shortfalls and other budget pressures. State and local spending on higher education hit a 25-year low in 2011, and nothing suggests a significant upturn in years to come. Schools have tried to make up the difference by raising tuition, but, for the first time, we're beginning to see significant buyer resistance. Federal money is still there, but it's not growing the way it once was, and with the federal government running massive deficits, any prospects of its gap filling also seem poor. So what will happen?

At first, of course, the answer will mostly be denial: short-term solutions, efforts to raise quick cash, and suggestions that what's going on is just temporary. Later there will be more significant changes, mostly aimed at cost cutting. (If experience is any guide, administration – especially sacred cows like diversity programs – will be cut last; actual teaching will be cut first.) Finally, there will be mergers and even outright closings of schools that can no longer operate. The schools that are left will be those that can survive in the new environment.

This won't be the end of higher education, of course, and the schools at the top of the food chain – the Ivy League and similar schools; top engineering schools like MIT, CalTech, and Georgia Tech; and the better flagship public universities – will survive at least comparatively unscathed. The transformation will nonetheless be wrenching. (Already, even some elite liberal-arts schools are facing credit downgrades as rating agencies doubt their business models, and that's just the beginning.)[15] Less-expensive alternative-education and certification schemes will arise, and existing institutions will do their best to marginalize and neutralize any newly arising schemes by employing everything from PR offensives to accrediting powers to outright legal assaults, but over time those assaults will largely fail.

In addition, administrators will – for as long as they can, anyway – resist making cuts to things that are priorities to administrators. They will, instead, cut spending elsewhere, even if doing so harms the overall mission of the school. They will change their behavior only when forced to.

We're already seeing some of this. Even as the once-mighty University of California system slashes programs and raises tuition, it has created a new systemwide "vice chancellor for equity, diversity, and inclusion." This is on top of the already enormous University of California diversity machine, which, as Heather Mac Donald notes, "includes the Chancellor's Diversity Office, the associate vice chancellor for faculty equity, the assistant vice chancellor for diversity, the faculty equity advisors, the graduate diversity coordinators, the staff diversity liaison, the undergraduate student diversity liaison, the graduate student diversity liaison, the chief diversity officer, the director of development for diversity initiatives, the Office of Academic Diversity and Equal Opportunity, the Committee on Gender Identity and Sexual Orientation Issues, the Committee on the Status of Women, the Campus Council on Climate, Culture and Inclusion, the Diversity Council, and the directors of the Cross-Cultural Center, the Lesbian Gay Bisexual Transgender Resource Center, and the Women's Center."[16]

While the UC system loses top cancer researchers to Rice University, it is creating new chaired professorships in, you guessed it, diversity studies. Likewise, in North Carolina, UNC-Wilmington is combining the physics and geology departments to save money, while diverting more funding to campus diversity offices.[17] This sort of thing illustrates the kind of priorities that emerge in a bubble that is not only financial but also intellectual. It will not survive in the new environment, though administrators will fight a grim rear-guard action as long as they are allowed, even though research suggests that the programs aren't doing much good, as students grow less, not more, committed to racial and gender equality the longer they are in college.[18]

As Mac Donald writes in *City Journal,* UC administrators' priorities aren't necessarily the public's:

The public knows about tuition increases but not about the unstoppable growth in the university's bureaucracy. Taxpayers may have heard about larger class sizes but not about the sacrosanct status of faculty teaching loads. Before the public decides how much more money to pour into the system, it needs a far better understanding of how UC spends the $22 billion it already commands. . . .

It's impossible to overstate the extent to which the diversity ideology has encroached upon UC's collective psyche and mission. No administrator, no regent, no academic dean or chair can open his mouth for long without professing fealty to diversity. It is the one constant in every university endeavor; it impinges on hiring, distorts the curriculum, and sucks up vast amounts of faculty time and taxpayer resources. The university's budget problems have not touched it. In September 2012, for instance, as the university system faced the threat of another $250 million in state funding cuts on top of the $1 billion lost since 2007, UC San Diego hired its first vice chancellor for equity, diversity, and inclusion. This new diversocrat would pull in a starting salary of $250,000, plus a relocation allowance of $60,000, a temporary housing allowance of $13,500, and the reimbursement of all moving expenses. (A pricey but appropriately "diverse" female-owned executive search firm had found this latest diversity accretion.) In May 2011, UCLA named a professional bureaucrat with a master's degree *in student-affairs administration as its first assistant dean for "campus climate," tasked with "maintaining the campus as a safe, welcoming, respectful place," in the words of UCLA's assistant vice chancellor and dean of students. In December 2010, UC San Francisco appointed its first vice chancellor of diversity and outreach – with a starting salary of $270,000 – to create a "diverse and inclusive environment," announced UC San Francisco chancellor Susan Desmond-Hellmann. Each of these new posts is wildly redundant with the armies of diversity functionaries already larding UC's bloated bureaucracy.*[19]

Diversity isn't the only sacred administrative cow, of course (though it's one of the most sacred), nor are diversity bureaucrats the only administrative locusts taking over the higher education system. The California State University system has more administrators than it has faculty,[20] and in this it is not alone. The University of Michigan has 53 percent more administrators than faculty,[21] and nationally, administrators are coming to outnumber faculty overall.

As Benjamin Ginsberg writes in the *Washington Monthly*:

Forty years ago, America's colleges employed more professors than administrators. The efforts of 446,830 professors were supported by 268,952 administrators and staffers. Over the past four decades, though, the number of full-time professors or "full-time equivalents" – that is, slots filled by two or more part-time faculty members whose combined hours equal those of a full-timer – increased slightly more than 50 percent. That percentage is comparable to the growth in student enrollments during the same time period. But the number of administrators and administrative staffers employed by those schools increased by an astonishing 85 percent and 240 percent, respectively.... Between 1975 and 2005, total spending by American higher educational institutions, *stated in constant dollars, tripled, to more than $325 billion per year. Over the same period, the faculty-to-student ratio has remained fairly constant, at approximately fifteen or sixteen students per instructor. One thing that has changed, dramatically, is the administrator-per-student ratio. In 1975, colleges employed one administrator for every eighty-four students and one professional staffer – admissions officers, information technology specialists, and the like – for every fifty students. By 2005, the administrator-to-student ratio had dropped to one administrator for every sixty-eight students while the ratio of professional staffers had dropped to one for every twenty-one students.*

Apparently, as colleges and universities have had more money to spend, they have not chosen to spend it on expanding their instructional resources – that is, on paying faculty. They have chosen, instead, to enhance their administrative and staff resources. A comprehensive study published by the Delta Cost Project in 2010 reported that between 1998 and 2008, America's private colleges increased spending on instruction by 22 percent while increasing spending on administration and staff support by 36 percent. Parents who wonder why college tuition is so high and why it increases so much each year may be less than pleased to learn that their sons and daughters will have an opportunity to interact with more administrators and staffers – but not more professors. Well, you can't have everything.... College administrations frequently tout the fiscal advantages of using part-time, "adjunct" faculty to teach courses. They fail, however, to apply the same logic to their own ranks. Over the past thirty years, the percentage of faculty members who are hired on a part-time basis has increased so dramatically that today almost half of the nation's professors work only part-time. And yet the percentage of administrators who are part-time employees has fallen during the same time period.[22]

The explosion of administrators is a major cause of college tuition increases, and when budgets are tight, cuts are often made in faculty hiring and salaries – but, somehow, there's always money for administrators, and the inevitable administrative conferences and meetings. Universities will resist cuts here too. At many schools, even as administrative staffs have ballooned, actual teaching has been farmed out to low-paid adjuncts, which is one reason faculty numbers have stayed largely flat.[23]

In private universities, pressure from donors may do something to streamline things. In public universities, we're likely to see increasing pressure from legislators to cut the administrative fat. And in both cases, parents – and prospective students – will provide pressure through resistance to tuition increases.

Of course, if you *really* wanted to do something about administrative bloat, the best approach would probably be to get the *U.S. News & World Report* to penalize schools in the rankings for having too many administrators – perhaps simply by awarding more points the leaner the administrator-to-faculty ratio is. But ultimately, budgetary pressures are likely to slim things down at least a bit.

For a time, many schools will try to maintain their enrollments by discounting tuition – disguised, usually, as increased financial aid – and, in fact, that is already happening. For the 2013–14 academic year, colleges offered unprecedented amounts of discounting, but many still had trouble filling their seats. As the *Wall Street Journal* reported:

> *Private U.S. colleges, worried they could be pricing themselves out of the market after years of relentless tuition increases, are offering record financial assistance to keep classrooms full.*
>
> *The average "tuition discount rate" – the reduction off list price afforded by grants and scholarships given by these schools – hit an all-time high of 45% last fall for incoming freshmen, according to a survey being released*

Monday [May 6, 2013] *by the National Association of College and University Business Officers.*

"It's a buyer's market" for all but the most select private colleges and flagship public universities, said Jim Scannell, president of Scannell & Kurz, a consulting firm in Pittsford, N.Y., that works with colleges on pricing and financial-aid strategies.

It is likely that some private colleges will be forced to be even more generous with discounts this fall. As of the May 1 deadline for many high-school seniors to commit for their freshman year of college, early reports suggest some non-top-tier schools fell 10% to 20% short of enrollment targets, said Mr. Scannell.

The jump in aid shows that many colleges are losing pricing power as more families focus on cost and value, with about 65% increasing their discount rate in the fall of 2012.[24]

This is really just price discounting (and price discrimination) disguised as charity, but there are limits to that approach. First of all, to the extent that they need tuition money to survive, schools won't be able to afford these discounts for long. Second, as more schools adopt this strategy, we're likely to see a race to the bottom. And third, once word of heavy discounting gets out, better-off parents who are expected to pay full freight – the higher education industry's cash cows – will feel like suckers and either demand discounts themselves or take their business elsewhere. Most "financial aid," after all, is just a form of price discrimination, allowing schools to set a price calculated to be the most the buyer can afford. (Imagine how car buying would be if the dealer got to know everything about your finances before making you an offer.) Parents who are paying full freight will resent that other students are getting the same product for less. Many already do, but expect them to become more vocal and active.

Some schools, like the University of the South at Sewanee,

have actually cut tuition, which turned out to increase enrollment and ultimately bring in more money. And other schools, like Ashland University, are now emulating Sewanee: Ashland has cut its 2014–15 tuition by 37%, more than $10,000.[25] Both Sewanee and others are now offering four-year tuition guarantees to attract price-shy students (and parents).[26] These are the early signs of a bubble deflating. Still, schools will have to set priorities in terms of enrollment size, tuition revenue, and "selectivity" measures that influence their all-important *U.S. News* rankings.

For the most vulnerable schools, the problem won't be one of priorities but of survival. Generally speaking, the most vulnerable schools will be those private schools with modest reputations and limited endowments – but with high tuitions. A generation or two in the past, such schools could maintain enrollment via legacies or, in some cases, religious affiliations. But when you're nearly as expensive as (or, in some cases, more expensive than) Harvard but without the reputation of Harvard, attracting students isn't as easy. And since schools with modest endowments can't supplement tuition income with endowment income, there will be sharp limits to their ability to cut their prices anyway, at least without engaging in dramatic cost cutting first. For them, things can only get worse.

I FOUGHT THE LAW (OF SUPPLY AND DEMAND), AND THE LAW WON

In some places, things are already worse. In my own world of legal education, the bubble has already burst. Law students who were willing, five years ago, to take on six-figure debt for a JD degree (in addition to whatever debt they had from college) are now much more reluctant to do so. Law-school applications have plummeted to pre-1985 levels – which is not surprising, given that average starting salaries have also plummeted to pre-1985 levels.[27] Worse yet, there are currently two law-school graduates for every legal job.[28] The drop in applications is thus colossal but unsurprising. In 2004 there were over 100,000 applicants to law school. The number for 2013 is just over 50,000.[29] As with most bubbles, the problem is that people just can't take on enough debt to keep it inflated, with tuitions rising so much faster than inflation. In 2001 the average private-law-school graduate carried $70,000 in debt; in 2011 it was $125,000.[30] This is despite the fact that salaries aren't rising, and employment prospects look much worse.

Students are rationally concluding that this much debt is dangerous, especially with the job market looking so iffy. And the impact is severe, as law professor William Henderson tells the *New York Times:*

> *"In the '80s and '90s, a liberal arts graduate who didn't know what to do went to law school," Professor Henderson of Indiana said. "Now you get $120,000 in debt and a default plan of last resort whose value is just too speculative. Students are voting with their feet. There are going to be massive layoffs in law schools this fall. We won't have the bodies we need to meet the payroll."[31]*

Or as another law professor puts it:

> *"Students are doing the math," said Michelle J. Anderson, dean of the City University of New York School of Law. "Most law schools are too expensive, the debt coming out is too high and the prospect of attaining a six-figure-income job is limited."[32]*

As this suggests, law schools are dealing with this decline in various ways. Some are reducing enrollment. (That's what we're doing at my law school, the University of Tennessee, and the University of Kansas law school has cut its first-year enrollment by a third.)[33] Reducing enrollment cuts tuition revenue while allowing schools to keep admission standards up so they aren't pushed down in the *U.S. News* rankings by admitting students with weaker credentials. While that's a valid approach for state schools that aren't tuition-dependent, it's too expensive for schools that depend on tuition revenue to keep the lights on. Meanwhile, faculty hiring has already fallen off dramatically, which was predictable. A couple of years ago, I spoke with a very smart former research assistant who had considered a career in legal academe, which would have required her to go back and get an LLM degree from a top-tier school like Yale or Stanford. When we spoke again more recently, she told me she had decided to stay in law practice. In her view, the future of legal academe wasn't bright enough to justify the investment, and she has turned out to be right.[34]

Some lower-tier private schools, with high tuition but low placement rates, are already offering staff buyouts, something we'll likely see more of.[35] If things continue to get worse, we'll probably see outright layoffs, and even tenured professors will not be immune.

These problems also ramify outward. At many schools – especially private universities – the law school serves as a major cash cow for the university as a whole. Law-school tuitions have traditionally been high, but legal education is comparatively cheap to provide: no special equipment, many large classes in which the cost of one professor is spread across many students, fewer expensive special programs. Often as much as 40 percent to 50 percent of law-school revenue winds up going to the university as a whole, which uses it to subsidize other programs.

How big a blow can a decline in law-school enrollment be? Consider this: declining revenue at Catholic University's law school caused the university *as a whole* to cut its budget by 20 percent.[36] It's not clear just how many, but many other private schools may be similarly dependent on law-school tuitions and may face serious problems if those decline. And even many taxpayer-supported public universities may nonetheless be creaming off substantial sums from law-school revenues –

sums that they will have to do without as the bubble bursts.

And, of course, it's not just law schools. Business schools are also facing decreasing applications for similar reasons, and so are many other graduate programs. Eventually, the same sort of logic that has produced declines in graduate programs is likely to cause people to rethink undergraduate education as well. If college graduates aren't getting jobs because of their degrees but instead are incurring substantial debt in getting them, sooner or later, behavior will change. Students – and not just law students – will be doing the math, and if the math looks bad enough, they'll find something else to do. Already, a smaller percentage of high school students are choosing to go on to college than just a few years ago.[37]

One ray of hope for undergraduate education is that, as has been widely noted, the generic college degree is today what a high school diploma used to be: a bare ticket to potential entry-level employment, even in fields that used to not require a college degree at all. It's reached the point where, as the *New York Times* reported, it often takes a BA degree to be hired as a file clerk:

> *The college degree is becoming the new high school diploma: the new minimum requirement, albeit an expensive one, for getting even the lowest-level job.*
>
> *Consider the 45-person law firm of Busch, Slipakoff & Schuh here in Atlanta, a place that has seen tremendous growth in the college-educated population. Like other employers across the country, the firm hires only people with a bachelor's degree, even for jobs that do not require college-level skills.*
>
> *This prerequisite applies to everyone, including the receptionist, paralegals, administrative assistants and file clerks. Even the office "runner" – the in-house courier who, for $10 an hour, ferries documents back and forth between the courthouse and the office – went to a four-year school.*[38]

But there's less long-term hope for undergraduate institutions than this might seem to indicate, as this vignette illustrates:

> *"I am over $100,000 in student loan debt right now," said Megan Parker, who earns −$37,000 as the firm's receptionist. She graduated from the Art Institute of Atlanta in 2011 with a degree in fashion and retail management, and spent months waiting on "bridezillas" at a couture boutique, among other stores, while churning out office-job applications.*
>
> *"I will probably never see the end of that bill, but I'm not really thinking about it right now," she said. "You know, this is a really great place to work."*[39]

In a lousy job environment, firms can get people with bachelor's degrees to do work that previously went to the uncolleged. But for those employees, the six-figure debt is a sunk cost. Will students really be willing to incur that debt to begin with if their best hope is a job that will never let them see the end of the toothache pain of indebtedness?

It seems doubtful. If an undergraduate degree – outside specialty areas like engineering or accounting – offers only the sort of jobs that high school diplomas used to offer, then it will ultimately be worth only the kind of investment that high school diplomas used to involve. People may not forgo college, but they will be unwilling to pay top dollar. Or even medium dollar.

The upshot is that higher education is facing a major structural change over the next decade or so, and the full impact is likely to strike sooner than most people expect. Change is coming, and it is unlikely to be either modest or gradual.

But how should people prepare for this change? Assume that I'm right, and that higher education – both undergraduate and graduate, including professional education like the law schools in which I teach – is heading for a major correction. What will that mean? What should people do? That's the next topic for discussion.

WHAT TO DO

Well, piece of advice No. 1 – good for pretty much all bubbles, in fact – is this: Don't go into debt. In bubbles, people borrow heavily because they expect the value of what they're borrowing against to increase.

In a booming housing market, for example, it makes sense to buy a house you can't quite afford, because it will increase in value enough to make the debt seem trivial, or at least manageable – as long as the market continues to boom. But there's a catch. Once the boom is over, all that debt is still there, but the return thereon is much diminished. And since the boom is based on expectations, things can go south with amazing speed once those expectations start to shift.

Right now, people are still borrowing heavily to pay the steadily increasing tuitions levied by higher education. But that borrowing is based on the expectation that students will earn enough to pay off their loans with a portion of the extra income their educations generate. Once people doubt that will happen, the bubble will burst. In addition, there's considerable evidence that the doubting is already well under way.

So my advice to students faced with choosing colleges (and graduate schools, and law schools) is simple: Don't go to colleges or schools that will require you to borrow a lot of money to attend. There's a good chance you'll find yourself deep in debt for no purpose. On the other hand, all that tuition discounting may mean that there will be bargains to be had. Just don't expect them to always be obvious bargains; you may have to research, and even dicker a bit, to get the best deal. Don't be afraid to dicker – schools may act like that's unheard of, but you won't be the only one.

And maybe you should rethink college entirely. According

to a recent report in the *Washington Post,* many people with college educations are already jumping the tracks to become skilled manual laborers: plumbers, electricians, and the like. It's easy to see why:

> *Apprentices start out getting paid half the scale for experienced workers, with raises every six months. Ultimately, many make as much or more as they would in jobs requiring a college degree. Licensed journeymen can expect to be paid $65,000 to $85,000 a year, depending on overtime.*
>
> *Local apprentice programs, which typically last five years, are swamped with applicants nowadays. The electricians' union program, for example, has 2,500 applications for 100 slots. And nearly 4,000 want to get one of the 300 slots at plumbers and pipe fitters school.*[40]

The problem is that class prejudice often keeps people out of these programs until they've already wasted years – and run up debts – in college:

> *"It's hard to get high school counselors to point anyone but their not-very-good students, or the ones in trouble, toward construction," said Dale Belman, a labor economist at Michigan State University. "Counselors want everyone to go to college. So now we're getting more of the college-educated going into the trades."*[41]

Nonetheless, people are noticing. And the Bureau of Labor Statistics predicts that 7 of the 10 fastest-growing jobs in the next decade will be based on on-the-job training rather than higher education.[42] (And they'll be hands-on jobs that are hard to outsource to foreigners: if you want your toilet fixed, it can't be done by somebody in Bangalore. In this sense, knowledge jobs, once touted as better than skilled trades – in Steve Earle's song, "Hillbilly Highway," his grandfather sent his father off to college so he could have a good job that would "use his brains and not his hands" – may now be less secure and less well compensated because "knowledge workers" and "symbolic analysts" are competing with everyone in the world, while your plumber is only competing with other plumbers within easy driving distance of your house.)[43] If the *Post* is right about this trend, a bursting of the bubble is growing likelier.

What about higher education folks? What should they (er, *we*) do? Well, once again, what can't go on forever, won't. And, increasingly, our work is looking more like that of an outsourced call-center worker than like that of a plumber. This should color our analysis.

For the past several decades, colleges and universities have built endowments, played *Moneyball*-style faculty hiring games, and constructed grand new buildings, while jacking up tuitions to pay for all these things (and, in the case of state schools, to make up for gradually diminishing public support). That has been made possible by an ocean of money borrowed by students – often with the encouragement and assistance of the universities. Business plans that are based on the continuation of this borrowing are likely to fare poorly.

Just as I advised students not to go into debt, my advice to universities is similar: Don't go on spending binges now that you expect to pay for with tuition revenues (or government aid) later. Those revenues may not be there as expected. (Some colleges have already gotten in trouble by borrowing money in the debt markets to support capital improvements for which state funding won't pay, only to face difficulty paying the money back.[44] Expect more of this down the line unless my advice here is followed.)

It's also time to think about curriculum reform and changes in instructional methods. Post-bubble, students are likely to be far more concerned about getting actual value for their educational dollars. Faced with straitened circumstances, colleges and universities will have to look at cutting costs while simultaneously increasing quality.

Online education – and programs focused more on things

that can help students earn more than on what faculty members want to teach – will help deliver more value for the dollar. In some areas, we may even see a move to apprenticeship models or other approaches that provide more genuine skills upon graduation.

But in traditional colleges, the first step is to ensure that students are actually learning useful things. This isn't much of a problem in engineering schools and the like, but in many other areas, core subjects have been shortchanged. A recent survey of more than 700 schools by the American Council of Trustees and Alumni found that many have virtually no requirements. Perhaps that's why students are studying 50 percent less than they were a couple of decades ago.

And a recent book, *Academically Adrift* by Richard Arum and Josipa Roksa, surveyed college students and found that there wasn't a lot of learning going on:

- 45 percent of students "did not demonstrate any significant improvement in learning" during the first two years of college.

- 36 percent of students "did not demonstrate any significant improvement in learning" over four years of college.[45]

Prices have been going up, but learning seems to have been going down. The primary reason, according to the study, is that courses aren't very rigorous. There's not much required of students, and the students aren't doing more than is required. If higher education is going to justify its cost, there needs to be a much bigger return on investment, which means much more actual learning, which means more rigorous course content and less fluff.

Though discussions of rigor often seem to devolve into commercials for science and engineering majors, there's plenty of room for rigor in liberal arts. I think the reason people often hold out engineering, etc., as examples of rigor is that the liberal arts, in general, have lost much more of their former rigor. But traditional liberal-arts skills – reading closely, analyzing, writing clearly – are not at all obsolete. They're just harder to find nowadays. I have a friend whose company hired two recent college grads, with degrees in marketing and journalism, basically to write product descriptions for catalogs, Amazon, and the like. She found that she had to go over their work repeatedly because even though they were recent college grads, they were incapable of writing clearly and within length limits. As I say, room for improvement.

Once this issue is addressed, there's plenty of room for improvement on the technological front. In the old days, professors were few, and it made sense for students to travel hundreds of miles to study with them. But today, once you move onto a campus, much of your learning, especially in the first couple of years, takes place in huge lecture halls where one professor addresses hundreds of students – or gets a teaching assistant to do it.

Some students are saving money by doing their first two years at community college. The quality of instruction is often better – and the classes smaller – than in four-year institutions where professors focus more on research than on teaching. That's a worthwhile strategy, but innovation at four-year institutions could help too. Now that webcasts are a routine feature of corporate training, perhaps it's time to make better use of the Web for education. Take the top teachers in a field and let students at multiple colleges access their lectures online. (Sure, there's not a lot of one-on-one interaction that way – but how much is there in a 200-student lecture class, really?) Once the basic information is covered, students can apply it in smaller advanced classes, in person. Would this save money? Possibly – and it would almost certainly produce better results.

The online approach is used by the popular Khan Academy, where students view lectures at their convenience and perfect their skills via video-game-like software, and the follow-up is done in a classroom, with a teacher's oversight. The idea behind this "flipped classroom" approach is to take advantage of mass delivery where it works best and to allow individualized attention where it helps most.

The Khan Academy has gotten a lot of attention, but it's not the last word in technological progress in education. Many for-profit online schools, such as Kaplan or Strayer University, are using their standardized course content and large enrollments to perform deep statistical analysis of how students perform and how changes in course content and course presentation can improve learning.[46] This is a knowledge base that is unavailable to traditional universities.

What's striking is that most of the potentially revolutionary change we're seeing has come from outside the educational establishment. Then again, breakthroughs often come from people working outside the old industries. As described earlier, Anya Kamenetz's *DIY U* talks about edupunks who are exploring unconventional thinking about teaching and learning. In fact, the best way to master many subjects may be for students to find their own path, with the role of the education establishment being more to certify competence than to actually teach. In one way, that's how it works already.

In moving ahead, though, we need to look beyond the gauzy, wishful thinking that has characterized a lot of talk about college. In his terrifically on-point – and hilarious – report on the absurdities of the college admissions process, *Crazy U*, Andrew Ferguson writes:

> *Beyond any one school the guides were propagandizing for the very idea of college, as the upper middle class conceives it – the embrace of leafy campuses, the raucous but mostly wholesome parties alongside the rigors of learning, the all-nighters and dorm-room camaraderie and late-night food runs.*[47]

Ferguson also notes that when it comes to college:

The subject entangles our deepest yearnings, our vanities, our social ambitions and class insecurities, and most profoundly our love and hopes for our children, with the largest questions of democracy, of equality, fairness, opportunity, the social good, even the nature of happiness.... The college mania won't subside anytime soon. Too many people, too many institutions and businesses have an interest, financial and ideological, in keeping it going. This was one of my many discoveries. Though not at all original to me, I took to dropping these mini-revelations at dinner parties, cocktail parties, school sporting events, my office, wherever parents with high school kids gathered. Facing the same trackless future my wife and I did, they scooped the nuggets like squirrels scurrying for acorns before winter set in.[48]

The squirrel analogy is a good one in a larger sense too. Much of the higher education bubble is driven not by hope or ambition but by fear. With economic insecurity abounding, many parents see college – especially an expensive, perhaps even a bit-beyond-their-means college – not so much as an investment as something more like status insurance. It's not really opportunity or fulfillment as such that they're after, but rather not-falling-out-of-the-middle-class insurance or, for the more hopeful, not-falling-out-of-the-upper-middle-class insurance. I was talking about this idea last year over drinks at the Union League Club in New York with a billionaire tech investor who's interested in education, and he said that in his opinion, most of the bubbles of the past few years have been more about fear than hope. The late-'90s tech bubble and early-2000s housing bubble, in his mind, were more about baby boomers who were afraid of not being able to retire than about hope for great wealth. The college bubble, he suggested, was another one, only based on parents' fear for their kids rather than themselves.

There's something to that, I think. But just as the tech and housing bubbles didn't solve the problems of those piling into Internet stocks or tract McMansions, so the college bubble isn't likely to provide the guarantees the pilers-in hope for. And, as with the other bubbles, getting carried away with the piling-in will make those problems worse for many.

It's also worth noting that while college can be great, the reality doesn't always live up to the gauzy fantasies. While some make friends, and memories, for a lifetime, others are lonely, depressed, and uncertain, drifting from major to major until eventually they graduate with whatever degree is easiest – and a lot of debt. Or, sometimes, they don't graduate at all but still have a lot of debt. For some, college is the beginning of problems with drugs, drinking, or sex that will cloud their adulthoods for years or even a lifetime.

College can even make income inequality worse, despite its being touted as the great equalizer. In a multiyear study of female college students, sociologists Elizabeth Armstrong and Laura Hamilton found that students who seemed similar in terms of "predictors" – grades and test scores – came out of college on very different trajectories. The biggest danger was when smart women from less well-off backgrounds got onto what Armstrong and Hamilton call the "party pathway." The richer girls who did this usually emerged okay, with family connections and parental subsidies allowing them to snag good jobs and internships in spite of any partying-related stumbles. The poorer girls with similar credentials ("strivers") who got on the party track tended to emerge with low GPAs, unimpressive post-college jobs (frequently jobs that they could have gotten without a college degree), and burdened with debt. They actually often wound up with downward mobility, rather than the upward mobility that colleges sell.[49] (Interestingly, the strivers who did best were the ones who transferred to less prestigious regional state universities, which were also often cheaper.[50] These schools – the Northern Kentucky Universities of the world – focus more on teaching and are often more oriented toward student success, frequently in a less party-oriented atmosphere.) The big schools, for the strivers, were often an expensive detour.

Some regarded these outcomes as false advertising on the part of the university. Armstrong and Hamilton quote the father of one of their strivers whose post-college prospects didn't live up to expectations:

> *It was a little deceptive, you know, in what they said and then what they produced. It's kind of like the stuff that works on TV and then you get it home and it doesn't really quite live up to the expectations.*[51]

In *Academically Adrift,* Arum and Roksa note, "Among students starting at four-year institutions, only 34 percent finish a bachelor's degree in four years, and barely two-thirds (64 percent) finish within six years."[52] The students who don't finish, of course, are still stuck with their student loans, meaning that college probably puts them in a worse economic position than if they'd simply taken a job out of high school. And the inequality enhancement isn't just financial:

> *In general, as we have shown, undergraduates are barely improving their CLA-measured skills in critical thinking, complex reasoning, and writing during their first two years of college. Even more disturbing, almost half are demonstrating no appreciable gain in these skills between the beginning of their freshman year and the end of their sophomore year. In addition to limited growth, learning in higher education is also unequal. Students from less educated families and racial/ethnic minority groups have lower levels of skills in critical thinking, complex reasoning, and writing (as measured by the CLA) as they enter college. These inequalities are largely preserved – or, in the case of African-American students, exacerbated – as students progress on their journeys through higher education.*[53]

They conclude, "Evidence of limited learning and persistent inequality should give pause to the recent emphasis on 'college for all' policies."[54] Indeed.

So while the traditional college approach works well for some – especially, I suspect, for the kinds of people who wind up as journalists or professors who write about higher education – it doesn't work for everyone. When you add to these failures its skyrocketing cost and the deadly danger of excessive student debt, it becomes clear that we ought to be thinking about alternatives. And in doing that, it's worth thinking about what a college degree is really for.

Right now, as noted, from an employer's standpoint a college degree is an expensive signifier that its holder has a basic ability to show up on time (mostly), to follow instructions (reasonably well), and to deal with others in close quarters without committing serious felonies. In some fields, it may also indicate important background knowledge and skills, but most students (even those in fields like engineering and accounting) will require further on-the-job training. An institution that could provide similar certification without requiring four (or more) years and a six-figure investment would have a huge advantage, especially if employers found that certification to be a more reliable indicator of competence than a college degree. Couple that with apprenticeship programs or internships, and you might not need college for many careers.

The major problem with this plan is that from students' and parents' perspectives, college now serves largely as a status marker, a sign of membership in the educated "caste," and as a place for people to meet future spouses of commensurate status. However, the sight of college graduates buried in debt may change that. We're already seeing signs of a shift in popular culture, with advice-column pieces and news articles appearing that discuss women and men whose huge student debt makes them unmarriageable.[55] At any rate, American culture at its best values people more for what they do than for their membership in a caste – and now seems like a good time to reassert that preference.

Perhaps online programs from prestigious schools will bridge the gap. MIT has already put many of its courses online,[56] and at present, you can learn from them, and even get certification, but there's no degree attached. It wouldn't be hard for MIT to add standard exams and a diploma, though, and if they do it right, an online degree from MIT might be worth a lot. Not as much as an old-fashioned MIT degree, perhaps, but quite possibly more than a degree from many existing brick-and-mortar schools. We're seeing the beginnings of an online revolution with accredited schools like Western Governors University.[57] There's also a new online startup, Minerva University, that aims to compete with elite brick-and-mortar schools, and it includes such big names as former Harvard President Larry Summers.[58]

Even more dramatically, the Georgia Institute of Technology, an engineering "public Ivy," has partnered with online educator Udacity to offer a master's degree in computer science. The cost? $7,000. And it's a real, accredited degree just like the ones that cost six times as much if earned on-campus. "This is a full-service degree," says Georgia Tech provost Rafael Bras. Though some faculty members are concerned that offering degrees online will dilute their exclusivity, Bras believes that if the degree's requirements are as rigorous, its value to employers – and degree-holders – will remain high.[59] At present, this is just a pilot project, dedicated to a single degree. But if it works, and it probably will, it's likely to be emulated in many other places, eventually for undergraduate programs as well. That, of course, will put further pressure on schools that cost more than their results can justify.

Writing in the *Wall Street Journal*, Andy Kessler sees the Georgia Tech initiative as a harbinger:

Consider what happened at San Jose State after the university last fall ran a test course in electrical engineering paid for by the Bill and Melinda Gates Foundation. Students who worked with online content passed at a higher rate than classroom-only students, 91% to 60%.

The course was so successful that the school's president decided to expand online courses, including humanities, which will also be rolled out to other California State universities....

I have nothing against teachers – or even high salaries, if the teachers are worth it. But half of recent college graduates don't have jobs or don't use their degree in the jobs they find. Since 1990, the cost of college has increased at four times the rate of inflation. Student loans are clocking in at $1 trillion.

Something's got to give. Education is going to change, the question is how and when. Think about it: Today's job market – whether you're designing new drugs, fracking for oil, writing mobile apps or marketing Pop Chips – requires graduates who can think strategically in real time, have strong cognitive skills, see patterns, work in groups and know their way around highly visual virtual environments. This is the same generation that grew up playing online games like Call of Duty *and* World of Warcraft, *but who are almost never asked to use their online skills in any classroom.*[60]

If this sort of thing takes off, we might eventually see a lot of people "going to college" without ever leaving home, but getting degrees that are more prestigious than current online degrees, which usually come from for-profit entities of modest reputation. Taking it a step further, though, we might separate the "going to college" part from the classes entirely. Online classes typically do that by giving you the classes without the college experience. But maybe there's also a market for the reverse.

Perhaps we'll even see the rise of "hoteling" for colleges. If people want the college experience of late-night dorm bull sessions, partying, and pizza, why not give it to them but outsource the actual teaching? Build a nice campus – or buy one, from a defunct traditional school – put in a lot of amenities, but don't bother hiring faculty: Just bring in your courses online, with engineering from Georgia Tech, arts and literature from Yale, business from Stanford, and so on. Hire some unemployed PhDs as tutors (there'll be plenty of those around, available at bargain-basement rates) and offer an unbundled college experience: *We provide the rock-climbing wall and Jacuzzis, the Ivy League provides the teaching!* It's a business model that just might work, especially in geographic locations students favor, and certainly many more-traditional higher-ed enterprises would have reason to fear it.

With fear, of course, comes resistance. Writing in the *New Yorker*, Nathan Heller talks about higher education's fear of change:

> *"Imagine you're at South Dakota State," he said, "and they're cash-strapped, and they say, 'Oh! There are these HarvardX courses. We'll hire an adjunct for three thousand dollars a semester, and we'll have the students watch this TV show.' Their faculty is going to dwindle very quickly. Eventually, that dwindling is going to make it to larger and less poverty-stricken universities and colleges. The fewer positions are out there, the fewer Ph.D.s get hired.*[61]

But writing in *The Atlantic*, Zachary Karabell responds that with student-loan debt ballooning and tuition climbing much faster than incomes, "College is going online, whether we like it or not."[62] According to Karabell:

> *Unquestionably, the next wave of online education will disrupt. It will threaten faculty and colleges, but it will empower students. Yes, we are a few years away from online courses providing degrees and credentials that will be seen by the marketplace as adequate. For now, taking courses online may enrich your life, but it will not provide the entrée into jobs requiring a degree, whether associate's or bachelor's. Many fields of graduate study will be untouched, but many others – law, accounting and others – are ripe for online credentializing.*

Having spent almost a decade as a graduate student and professor, I was always struck by how resistant to change and questioning academic cabals could be. The growth of online education is yet another example. Many are embracing it, and many are resisting it because it represents change to a world that often moves at the pace of medieval guilds.

The beneficiaries, however, are students, which really means all of us. The costs of obtaining needed credentials will plummet, and the ability to create more tailored, vocational programs aligned with the skills employers need will increase exponentially. That will likely lead to some shrinkage in the number of physical institutions offering degrees, but an increase in the number of people obtaining them. It will also mean that those taking on debt – especially at elite schools – will be those most likely to be able to bear those debts, while those who need more specific and vocational education for decently paid but not high-paying jobs will not be saddled with loans out of proportion to their earning potential.[63]

Benefits for the masses, paid for by stripping perquisites from the privileged. This sounds like the sort of thing that faculties have been advocating for years in society at large, though generally at others' expense. But now it may be higher education's turn to sacrifice for the common good.

Meanwhile, for the states, and big donors, who fund those portions of higher education that the students don't, a post-bubble world will bring some changes too. Many states have been cutting aid to higher education, content to let higher tuition pick up the slack.

Some may choose to change that by boosting state subsidies (if they can afford it), but regardless, I expect more direct oversight of state institutions from those who fund them. Public universities' priorities will be brought closer to states' priorities, and we can expect more outside pressure for increased rigor and fewer courses and majors in areas that seem to be more about politics or trendiness than substance. We can also expect resistance from those faculty and administrators with investments in those fields, but it is unlikely to prevail as the money runs out.

For private schools, government oversight is less direct – but to an even greater extent than state schools, private institutions have been dependent on a flood of government-guaranteed credit, and they are likely to see more scrutiny as well if that is to continue.

As former British Prime Minister Margaret Thatcher famously remarked, the problem with socialism is that you eventually run out of other people's money, and that's likely to be the problem facing higher education too: not enough of other people's money.

One reform that would be useful at both public and private institutions is budget transparency. University budgets are notoriously byzantine, and administrators generally like it that way. But a movement for budget transparency, spearheaded in Oregon, would put transparency in the hands of, well, anyone.

Several years ago, Oregon implemented a system involving a website, updated daily, that shows where every dollar is spent. The result: "It means that students, parents, and the taxpaying public can finally discover (say) how much that new ornamental gate for the baseball stadium actually cost, and to whom the money was paid (a legislative crony, the coach's brother-in-law, or an honest local business). It means the public can finally see how much money was spent redecorating the chancellor's bedroom, or putting up the football team in a local hotel the night before a home (!) game, as is done at many big universities in the U.S., believe it or not. And when more than one campus operates a system like this, it means explicit comparisons can be made from one institution to another."[64] This is the sort of transparency that taxpayers should demand for public universities – and, maybe, even for private universities that receive significant amounts of public money, as nearly all do.

Finances aren't the only thing. Graduation rates, employment after graduation, loan default rates, and so on are likely to get a lot more attention. Institutions may even be forced to absorb some of the cost of student-loan defaults, as an incentive not to encourage students to take on more debt than they can repay, or to major in fields in which employment prospects are dim. What would a serious student-loan reform look like? Well, it would look more like normal loans. Students' ability to borrow would be based on the likelihood that they'd be able to pay. Plus, loans would be dischargeable in bankruptcy if things turned out badly.

Right now, student loans are sold on the basis that "college" promotes higher earnings. But "college" isn't an undifferentiated product. Some degrees – say, in electrical engineering – increase earnings dramatically. Others – in, say, gender studies – not so much. A rational lender would be much more willing to finance the former than the latter.

Oh, and in ordinary credit transactions, creditors bear some risk. Lend someone money that they can't pay back, and you take a loss if they go bankrupt. In the housing bubble, this discipline broke down because the people writing the loans weren't going to hold onto the mortgages. Similarly, colleges today get their money up front; if the student can't pay it back, that's someone else's problem (mostly the student's – and the taxpayers').

Let's give colleges some skin in the game by making *them* absorb the loss, or at least part of it, if students can't pay. Perhaps if students can't pay their loans by 10 years after graduation, they should be allowed to discharge them in bankruptcy, with the institutions that got the loan money on the hook for, say, 20 percent of the loss. You fix a malfunctioning credit system by ensuring that the people who can control the risks are the ones who face a loss if things go wrong. Our student-loan system as it exists today puts all the risk onto the students and taxpayers, who are the least-informed parties in the borrowing transaction. That should change.

Finally, for the entrepreneurs out there, this bubble-bursting may be an opportunity. One of the underpinnings of higher education, as mentioned above, is its value as a credential to employers. A college degree demonstrates, at least, moderate intelligence – and, as noted, perhaps more importantly the ability to show up and perform on a reasonably reliable basis, something that is of considerable interest when hiring people, a surprisingly large number of whom (as most employers can attest) do neither. But a college degree is an expensive way to get an entry-level credential. New approaches to credentialing, approaches that inform employers more reliably while costing less than a college degree, are likely to become increasingly appealing over the coming decade.

If I were an employer, I'd find a reliable non-college-based credentialing system pretty appealing. First, it wouldn't have to be all that great to be a more reliable indicator of knowledge and skills than a typical college diploma. Second, all things being equal, I'd much rather hire someone who wasn't burdened by six-figure debt: such employees are likely to be more cheerful, less financially stressed (which can lead to problems with embezzlement and worse) and, significantly, willing to work for less since they don't have big student-loan payments to cover.

What's more, someone who successfully completes a rigorous program online is likely to be more self-disciplined and more of a self-starter than someone who completes college in the traditional fashion. For a lot of employers, that's sure to be a significant plus.

So there's a need for an alternative credentialing system. Filling that need will make someone rich. To any entrepreneurs reading this, good luck. And once you hit it big, please remember the impecunious law professor who put this idea in your head.

*   *   *

POLITICS

Wrenching economic change is easy to endure, as long as it's happening to other people. Thus, as blue-collar workers suffered the pangs of economic transitions in the 1980s and 1990s, it was easy for white-collar workers and academics to talk about the benefits of globalization and of technological progress in the workplace. They may have been right about all that, but don't expect academics to be so enthusiastic when their jobs are being eliminated and their pay is being cut.

The bursting of the higher education bubble is pretty much inevitable, being a product of economic forces that politics cannot control. But that doesn't mean that there won't be a political firestorm or two along the way. And while politics won't prevent the bubble's bursting, the political response can make a big difference in how well things go. What kinds of responses can we expect?

At one end of the spectrum, we may see the sort of diehard job protection that we've seen in other shrinking sectors, where the focus is on (1) keeping competition down for as long as possible; and (2) preserving the jobs, perks, and salaries of senior workers at all costs. If that is the main response, we'll see bitterly contested efforts to use accrediting agencies and other gatekeepers to block the rise of new, lower-cost approaches to higher education. At the same time, we'll see existing tenured faculty fighting to retain their positions, while new academic hires become non-tenure-track contract appointments. (Already, many universities have turned many or most introductory courses over to low-paid adjuncts or visiting professors who don't have tenure and, in many cases, don't get health or retirement benefits.) In the short term, this will reduce the pain for faculty members and administrators, but the end result will be a hollowed-out university.

At the other end, we may see serious efforts to rebuild the higher education model. Instead of looking at what faculty want and then telling students that's what they get, we may instead look at what skills and knowledge students need to possess after graduation – and can afford to pay for – and structure programs accordingly.

In practice, of course, it won't be an either/or thing. Because higher education is decentralized, we'll see all sorts of different responses. Some will succeed and some will fail. Those who learn from the experience of others will be better able to make their own choices. Those who don blinders will learn only from their own experience, which may well turn out to be bitter.

Where state institutions are concerned, there will be an opportunity for the public to take a hand, if people are interested. Ordinarily, the running of state universities is left to administrators and trustees, with perhaps a bit of attention from the legislature, mostly where budgets are concerned. But as things begin to change, new ideas from outside will get a hearing.

Interested citizens should consider attending trustees' meetings, talking to legislators, and in general making noise about the priorities of state institutions – and whether they are serving the public or not. Does it make sense to cut science funding while expanding diversity programs? Is a new gym or stadium really a top priority? It is quite possible that we will see a broad-based popular movement for higher education reform. University spokespeople have been telling us for years that higher education is a matter of public interest. It should not be surprising if the public becomes interested as it becomes clear that the existing model has failed. My advice to outside agitators: Master the arcana of the budget process. Even many university administrators don't really understand how it works.

Private institutions do not enjoy (if that is the word) the same degree of outside scrutiny – but here too, alumni, students, parents, and other interested parties will have more of a chance to weigh in than has been usual. And, given that private institutions are actually more dependent on federal student-loan money than state institutions are, they will be particularly subject to pressures for reform that are tied to eligibility to receive federal funds.

Students and prospective students will have an effect – and, indeed, already are doing so – simply by becoming better informed and less willing to pay top dollar for an inferior product. Ultimately, you can't run a college if you can't fill the seats with paying students, and that will be harder and harder to do for schools that don't produce visible value, particularly as college enrollments are already declining, with 2012 enrollment a half-million below that of 2011.[65] Those schools that get ahead of the curve here will prosper, while those that lag behind will not.

There will likely be at least one major effort to secure federal bailout money for the higher education sector, but the prospects for that relief seem poor. The nation is already in sad financial shape, and higher education already received a substantial slug of "stimulus" money in 2009 that was mostly used to conduct business as usual for a bit longer. Should another bailout occur, its impact is likely to be similarly short-lived. At any rate, ironically enough, the social programs that many academics have long supported now represent much more powerful political interest groups, meaning that in the competition for scarce resources, higher education is likely to find itself outnumbered and outgunned by other claims on the public fisc.

But that's okay. The higher education bubble isn't bursting because of a shortage of money. It is bursting because of a shortage of value. The solution is to improve the product, not to increase the subsidy.

SOME FUTURE SCENARIOS

So what will happen? There are several possibilities:

1. SHRINKAGE. It's possible that higher education will simply contract until it's down to a level that can support itself. How much contraction will that involve? It's

hard to say. In the legal academy, we're graduating about twice as many people as there are legal jobs for them. But nobody expects half the law schools in America to go out of business. College outcomes are more imprecise, and people go to college for a lot of reasons. But if the main reason people go to college is economic – and, at any rate, that's the main way college is sold, as an "investment" – then there are a lot of people graduating from college now for whom the investment is a poor one. If those people leave higher education, a lot of colleges and universities will shrink or go out of business.

2. RECONFIGURATION. Of course, it may be that people won't quit college but rather will just pursue it differently. After all, if you want to improve return on investment, there are two ways to go about it: You can increase the return while keeping the investment the same, or you can reduce the investment while keeping the return the same. So if all you're looking to do is recoup the basic, ticket-punching college-degree-as-diploma return for a college education, then the thing to do is to get that education as cheaply as possible. People who have this in mind might go online or to a community college and then to the cheapest state institution they can get into. (This may be better in other ways too. Note that the strivers in the Armstrong/Hamilton study did better in regional state universities.) If widely adopted, this won't cut college enrollment that much as a whole, but it will pull a lot of students out of schools that cost too much for the value of their degrees. Those schools will have to change, or die. Even if you need a college degree to get a $37,000 receptionist job, a $37,000 job with no student-loan debt is vastly preferable to a $37,000 job with $100,000 in student-loan debt.

3. SUBSTITUTION. People might pursue certificates in valuable skills – computer security, welding, whatever – instead of bachelor's degrees. If a lot of people do this,

the overall college population will shrink, and many institutions will suffer. On the other hand, there's another kind of substitution we might see: if what people are looking for from college isn't a degree but a social experience, perhaps they will find better ways to get a peer-bonding experience without dropping six figures and running into debt. Burning Man or Bonnaroo are a lot cheaper than college, and then there's the prospect of taking a *Wanderjahr* or doing foreign charity work. Compared with $125,000 in debt for a degree in women's and religious studies, that doesn't sound too bad. There are business opportunities here for the entrepreneurially minded.

4. EXIT. While it's harder than it used to be to get ahead in America, even with a college degree, it's probably easier (and more comfortable) than ever to just barely get by. For some, the appeal of cheap living – with Internet porn, video games, weekend parties, and occasional hookups – will make subsistence-level jobs seem adequate, making a college degree superfluous. These people may not be getting ahead, but they won't be buried in debt, either. Nor will they stay up at night worried about the "toothache pain" of student-loan payments. That might make a resurgence of slacker culture look more appealing.

5. NEW MODELS. It's possible that people will find entirely new ways to meet the needs that are currently being met by higher education, ways currently unforeseeable, or at least unforeseen. The chances of this happening are actually pretty good. There are a lot of smart people thinking about the problem, and what they come up with may be as hard to predict today as Facebook or Twitter were in 1993.

What all the above scenarios have in common, though, is that traditional higher education won't be as flush in coming years as it has been over the past few decades. That, alas, seems like a safe prediction, whatever transpires. Something that can't go on forever, won't.

BUBBLES ARE INEVITABLE

There's nothing evil or unnatural about a bubble, or about the people who participate in one. Bubbles are an inevitable part of human nature and appear in almost every field of endeavor. When bubbles burst, it's painful – but the sources of the pain lie not so much in the bust as in the poor decisions made during the preceding boom. Resources were allocated in ways that didn't make sense, because the bubble made them *seem* to make sense for a while. It's the consequences of that misallocation that account for the pain.

And it's not the end of the world when a bubble bursts, either. When the tech bubble burst, people lost money (some people lost a *lot* of money) and some people lost jobs, but the Internet didn't go away, and neither did Internet businesses. Likewise, the bursting of the higher education bubble won't mean the end of higher education. It'll just mean that there will be less "dumb money" out there to be harvested.

But inevitably, change will come, and that's not so bad. This is the 21st century. It's not shocking to think that higher education will go through major changes over the coming decade or two. What would be shocking is if things were to stay the same, when rapid change has been the norm in every other knowledge-based industry lately.

I don't pretend to know how it will all work out, but I hope the thoughts in this section have been useful to readers, and I encourage you to join in the conversation in the years to come.

Education

In the previous section, I wrote about a higher education bubble – the notion that America is spending more than it can afford on higher education, driven by the kind of cheap credit (and mass infatuation) that fueled the housing bubble. But even as the higher education bubble begins to deflate, I think we're also starting to see the deflation of what might be called a lower education bubble – that is, the constant flow over decades of more and more money into K-12 education without any significant degree of buyer resistance, in spite of the often low quality of the education it purchases.

The leading case in point here is the battle over public-employee unions in Wisconsin and elsewhere, which bodes poorly for the state of lower education. Wisconsin spends a lot of money on education, and its teachers are well paid. The average total compensation for a teacher in Milwaukee public schools is more than $100,000 per year. In fact, Wisconsin spends more money per pupil than any other state in the Midwest. Nonetheless, two-thirds of Wisconsin eighth-graders can't read proficiently.

But it gets worse. "The test also showed that the reading abilities of Wisconsin public-school eighth-graders had not improved at all between 1998 and 2009 despite a significant inflation-adjusted increase in the amount of money Wisconsin public schools spent per pupil each year," according to CBS News. "From 1998 to 2008, Wisconsin public schools increased their per pupil spending by $4,245 in real terms yet did not add a single point to the reading scores of their eighth-graders and still could lift only one-third of their eighth-graders to at least a 'proficient' level in reading."[1]

So it's lots of pay but not much in the way of performance. Wisconsin's situation is, alas, typical of public education at the K-12 level around the country. (In fact, one of the reasons given for the increase in higher education costs is the need to provide remedial education for many high school graduates who never managed to learn the things they were supposed to have learned before they arrived at college. It's a shaky explanation for high college costs, but the phenomenon itself is beyond dispute.)

So at the K-12 level, we've got an educational system that in many fundamental ways hasn't changed in 100 years – except, of course, by becoming much less rigorous – but that nonetheless has become vastly more expensive without producing significantly better results.

In the past, when problems with education were raised, the solution was always to spend more money. Again, as economist Herbert Stein famously noted, something that can't go on forever, won't. Steady increases in per-pupil spending without any commensurate increase in learning can't go on forever. So they won't. And as state after state faces near bankruptcy (and, in the case of some municipalities, *actual* bankruptcy), we've pretty much hit that point now.

So what does that mean? Well, in the short term, it means showdowns like the one in Wisconsin, where the folks who received those big increases in the past spent over a year raging against the drying up of the government teat. Getting rid of teachers unions and overgenerous, underfunded public pensions is something many states will have to do to remain solvent. But that's just the short term. Over the longer term – which means, really, the next five to 10 years at the most – straitened circumstances and the need for better education will require more significant change.

When our public education system was created in the 19th century, its goal, quite explicitly, was to produce obedient and orderly factory workers to fill the new jobs being created by the Industrial Revolution. Those jobs are mostly gone now, and the needs of the 21st century are not the needs of the 19th. Perhaps there's still a role for teaching children to sit up straight and form lines, but perhaps not, and this role for public education is undoubtedly less important than it once was. Certainly the rapidly increasing willingness of parents to try homeschooling, charter schools, online schools, and other alternative approaches suggests that a lot of people are unhappy with the status quo.

Like striking steelworkers in the 1970s, today's teachers' immediate unhappiness may come from reductions in benefits. But their bigger problem is an industry that hasn't kept up with the times and isn't producing the value it once did. Until that changes, we're likely to see deflation of the lower education bubble as well as the higher. In the coming pages, we'll see how.

IN THE BEGINNING

Traditionally, education was not considered the domain of the state. From ancient times, wealthy and middle-class families hired tutors for their children; other schooling was typically provided by parents and religious organizations. For most people, learning was on the job, and they started as children and gradually picked up knowledge about specific skills – farming, shoemaking, merchandising, whatever – along the way. There might be a formal apprenticeship structure, or there might not be. Beyond basic arithmetic and writing skills (if that), not much in the way of formal academic training was needed, or obtained, except among the elites (and not all of them).

With the Industrial Revolution, things changed. Industrial-age factories needed workers with more knowledge – and the rapid change brought about by technological progress meant that they needed more abstract skills too. At the same time, older workers didn't want to compete with low-priced child labor, while the Victorian era's more-sentimental attitudes toward children made the idea of factory work by kids seem barbaric.

The result was the growth of publicly financed and, more significantly, publicly operated school systems. As Seth Godin writes:

> *Part of the rationale used to sell this major transformation to industrialists was the idea that educated kids would actually become more compliant and productive workers. Our current system of teaching kids to sit in straight rows and obey instructions isn't a coincidence – it was an investment in our economic future. The plan: trade short-term child-labor wages for longer-term productivity by giving kids a head start in doing what they're told.*
>
> *Large-scale education was not developed to motivate kids or to create scholars. It was invented to churn out adults who worked well within the system. Scale was more important than quality, just as it was for most industrialists.*
>
> *Of course, it worked. Several generations of productive, fully employed workers followed. But now?*[2]

Industrial Revolution schooling involved Industrial Revolution goals and Industrial Revolution methods – organization, standardization, and an overall assembly-line approach. In fact, the industrial-era public school (which persists to the present) is basically an assembly line: kindergartners come in at one end; graduates with diplomas emerge at the other. Each year they advance to the next stage (grade), where the next group of assembly workers (teachers) performs the standardized tasks (curricula) to advance the product (students) to the next assembly stage (grade). Eventually, they roll off the assembly line and into the marketplace at graduation.

And, as Godin notes, it worked. The growth of widespread public education in the United States was one of the great accomplishments of the late 19th and early 20th century project of elevating the lower classes into a broad-based middle class. It's possible, of course, that we might have accomplished the same thing without government-run schools (literacy rates, as we have seen, were very high in colonial America), but it's by no means certain, and doing so in the face of a flood of immigrants, many of whom spoke little or no English, probably would have taken longer and been less encompassing.

But while it worked then, Godin's other question – "But now?" – is the question for our age. And in a way, it should be no surprise if the next decade or so marks major change. Education is a knowledge industry, after all, and why should we expect a knowledge industry in the 21st century to succeed by following a model pioneered in the 19th? As Godin says, "Every year, we churn out millions of workers who are trained to do 1925-style labor." That won't work when kids in first grade as this is being written will be on the job market in 2025.

The current system isn't working. And, alas, neither are too many of its graduates. There may be a connection.

THE PROBLEM

It's no secret that existing schools are underperforming. We keep putting more money and resources into them, but we keep getting poorly educated students out of them.

In 1983 – three decades ago – the report *A Nation at Risk* was published by President Reagan's National Commission on Excellence in Education and famously observed, "If an unfriendly foreign power had attempted to impose on America the mediocre educational performance that exists today, we might well have viewed it as an act of war."[3] Since then, things have, if anything, gotten worse. But in the essentials, not much has changed.

There are a lot of reasons for this stagnation. Parents with children care about education, but, for the most part, by the time they become aware of problems, it's too late for them to agitate for change in time to benefit their own kids. It's easier to exit the system in favor of private schools, homeschooling, or even just a better school district (though the last option usually requires moving) than it is to effect change. Then, too, many parents value school as much as a place to send their kids while they're at work as for any educational benefit. *Those* parents are easy to satisfy. But that's not the only barrier to improvement.

Unsurprisingly, the industrial model of public education has led to an industrial model of labor, complete with powerful unions that make many changes more difficult. In the 1930s, the economist John Hicks famously wrote, "The best of all monopoly profits is a quiet life."[4] Change is uncomfortable, and teachers – and, for that matter, administrators – value their own comfort.

There's also a strong current of nostalgia. Parents tend to like the idea of their children's education recapitulating their own. There may be an evolutionary component to that – the cavemen who wanted their children to learn the things they did about finding food and avoiding cave bears were probably more likely to see their genes survive to the next generation – but it's not so adaptive today. Today's parents, after all, are of an age to be products of the very schools that *A Nation at Risk* called "an act of war."[5] Why recapitulate *that?*

In the 19th century, we needed obedient factory employees who had enough education to execute instructions that were designed by their betters. Today those jobs have mostly gone to China (or to Bangladesh). So we should probably be teaching new and different things. Today's schools, however, aren't even successfully teaching the basics.

There are other negatives. Putting kids together and sorting by age also created that dysfunctional modern creature, the "teenager." Once, teenagers weren't so much a demographic as adults in training. They worked, did farm chores, watched children, and generally functioned in the real world. They got status and recognition for doing these things well, and they got shame and disapproval for doing them badly.

But once they were segregated by age in public schools, teens looked to their peers for status and recognition instead of to society at large. As Thomas Hine writes in *American Heritage,* "Young people became teenagers because we had nothing better for them to do. We began seeing them not as productive but as gullible consumers."[6] Not surprisingly, the kinds of behaviors that gain teenagers status from other teenagers differ from the kinds of things that gain teenagers status from adults: early sex, drinking, and a variety of other "cool" but dysfunctional characteristics – once frowned upon – now become the keys to popularity. When teenagers are herded together and separated by age, those behaviors gain in salience, and at considerable cost.

This is a phenomenon described in considerable detail by psychologists Joseph Allen and Claudia Worrell, in their *Escaping the Endless Adolescence: How We Can Help Our Teenagers Grow Up Before They Grow Old.*[7] Although, they report, we're often told that teenagers have "always been this way" and that they're overly influenced by "hormones" or the "teenage brain," the fact is that the modern teenager is a modern phenomenon, and teenagers in previous eras were far more responsible – and far more integrated into society as a whole. A hundred years ago, they note, teenagers "were not only essential to making a household run each day, but contributed almost a third of the family's total household income." Today's teenagers, on the other hand, are largely consumers, not producers, something that now continues through college and even afterward. The resulting immaturity, they say, makes age 25 look like the new 15. Is that good? No, they report. This extended disconnection from the real world, at a time when people are, in many ways, at the height of their physical and mental powers, creates stress. "The average college student now reports as much anxiety as did the average *psychiatric patient* forty years ago," they write.[8] And although schoolwork can be demanding, students know that it's, in an important sense, not real.

Allen and Worrell contrast school with the experience of a man named Pete who worked as a teenager in a men's clothing store in New Hampshire in the 1970s, where he was the youngest employee by twenty years. The work wasn't exciting, but people depended on him to get it right:

> *"Even at age fifteen I knew that folding shirts was kind of trivial," he recalls. "Whether or not I flicked the cuffs in onto themselves just right to make them lie flat, I knew was not a life-changing event. What was a life-changing event was that I realized that these 'men's men' weren't going to consider me one of their club until I knew how to do it correctly, and I demonstrated that I could be relied upon to do it correctly again and again, because to them, even though they knew they were working in a relatively inconsequential job, this was the way that they displayed their pride, their craftsmanship. They let me know that it was important that I shared this focus, or I would never be trusted to be in the club. . . . This job also made me see that it was important that, every day, I show up, and on time because these guys were waiting to take their own break until I covered one of them in the store. So my being there was not some silly after-school job. It was, I began to see, a small cog in what made that place successful. . . . For me, that first job was a permanent character builder. It taught me: Show up on time. Do what you say you are going to do. Finish what you begin."[9]*

Allen and Worrell note, "These adult men had become Pete's peer group." After working there for a while, he reports, "I lost a bit of interest in gaining acceptance from my peers and realized that it was much more fun and more interesting to gain acceptance from people who you can learn a lot more from."[10] Pete was lucky because he got to experience something that too many kids don't get to experience today – real work, outside school, with real adults.

Of course, as the authors also note, not all work is equally character building. Although fast-food jobs can be a surprisingly rapid path to success for the motivated, most teenagers who start a fast-food job find themselves supervised by, basically, slightly older teenagers. This isn't the same thing as working with mature adults.

In *The Case Against Adolescence,* psychologist Robert Epstein makes similar observations. Noting that teens, who used to be treated more like adults, are now so hedged about with restrictions that in California, they have to be 18 to have a paper route, he writes, "It's likely that the turmoil we see among teens is an unintended result of the artificial extension of childhood."[11] Modern adolescence, he observes, is a modern invention, and most of the restrictions on teenagers that we take for granted are actually fairly recent in nature. Taking away the opportunity for teenagers to behave responsibly and earn respect from nonpeers just ensures the growth of a toxic "peer culture" that values appearance over achievement and rule breaking over responsibility.

Furthermore, nowadays that isolation from the adult world extends well beyond high school. Students in high school may now forgo work – if such work exists – so they can concentrate on grades, AP exam scores, and extracurricular activities (many basically bogus) aimed at getting them into a good college. Then, once in college, they may be encouraged not to work so as to focus on grades. In some sense, these may be wise moves, but in another, they mean that people can graduate from college at 22 – or, increasingly, 23, 24, or 25 – without ever having really been in an adult-focused environment. Twenty-five really can be the new 15. Ironically, says Epstein, the evidence is that teens, given meaningful tasks, are just as capable of handling responsibility as most adults – who themselves can be irresponsible if treated like children. But "like children" is how our K-12 system (and, all too often these days, college) treats young people.[12]

An education system that provides more opportunities for the kind of interaction that Pete enjoyed, above, would do more to build character and the kinds of skills that lead to real-life achievement. But, as Epstein notes, there are a lot of people who benefit from keeping teens infantilized. That includes people in our ever more expensive K-12 education system.

What's more, as we've increased the amount of money going in, there's been no corresponding increase in learning. One reason for that is that a disproportionate amount of money has gone into administration, rather than to teaching. According to a report in the Education Gadfly describing a study by Benjamin Scafidi called *The School Staffing Surge: Decades of Employment Growth in America's Public Schools*, "Between 1950 and 2009, the number of K-12 public school students increased by 96 percent. During that same period, the number of full-time equivalent (FTE) school employees grew by 386 percent. Of those personnel, the number of teachers increased by 252 percent, while the ranks of administrators and other staff grew by 702 percent – more than 7 times the increase in students."[13]

These education administrators don't teach; if anything, they create excess paperwork for the people who do. Some of them, of course, are required to do so by federal regulations, but that hardly improves the situation on the ground. This is one reason more money hasn't improved things: it's not going to teaching but to paper pushing. As Robert Maranto and Michael McShane write:

In constant dollars, education spending rose from $1,214 in 1945 to just under $10,500 in 2008. The St. Louis public schools, for example, spend more than $14,000 per student per year, so if it has problems, money is not one of them. What's far more important is how that money is spent.... While expenditures have been increasing over the past several decades, performance has not. The

National Assessment of Educational Progress has been given to a representative sample of U.S. students since the early 1970s, and the results have been basically flat. Similarly, the graduation rate for students has remained stagnant, as well, at about 75 percent nationwide. While some might argue that students today are somehow more expensive to educate, it should be noted that in this time period, rates of child poverty have declined and, in theory, technological advances should have been able to automate and thus decrease the price of some of the processes of schooling.[14]

As with higher education, the problem isn't a shortage of money. The problem is a shortage of value. That is illustrated in the following charts.

First, the United States spends more than many nations whose schools produce better performance.

FIGURE 1. K-12 SPENDING IN THE OECD

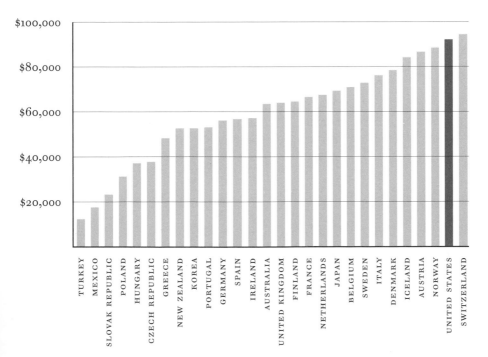

Second, while costs have increased dramatically, performance has not improved.

FIGURE 2. REAL COST OF K-12 PUBLIC EDUCATION AND PERCENTAGE CHANGE IN ACHIEVEMENT IN 17-YEAR-OLDS

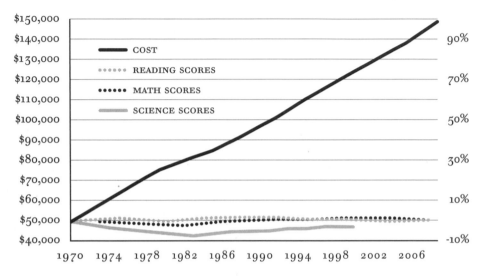

Third, pursuing the politicians' panacea – smaller class sizes – hasn't helped.

FIGURE 3. STUDENT–TEACHER RATIOS IN U.S. PUBLIC SCHOOLS

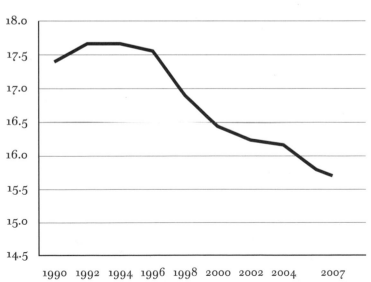

Adding teachers and administrators has benefited unions (more members) and politicians who draw support from those unions (more voters beholden to them), and it has cost a lot of money. What it hasn't done is conferred any measurable benefit on students, who are supposed to be the beneficiaries of public education. And now people have started to notice.

The result is that parents and taxpayers are losing faith in public education. And that portends a potential implosion.

THE COMING IMPLOSION

The *New York Times* reports that America's largest school districts are seeing devastating drops in enrollment:

> *Enrollment in nearly half of the nation's largest school districts has dropped steadily over the last five years, triggering school closings that have destabilized neighborhoods, caused layoffs of essential staff and concerns in many cities that the students who remain are some of the neediest and most difficult to educate. . . .*
>
> *In some cases, the collapse of housing prices has led homeowners to stay put, making it difficult for new families – and new prospective students – to move in and take their place.*
>
> *But some say the schools are partly to blame. "We have record-low confidence in our public schools," said Kevin Johnson, the mayor of Sacramento and head of education policy for the United States Conference of Mayors. . . . "If we have high-quality choices in all neighborhoods, you don't have that exodus taking place," he said.*
>
> *The rise of charter schools has accelerated some enrollment declines. The number of students fell about 5 percent in traditional public school districts between 2005 and 2010; by comparison, the number of students in all-charter districts soared by close to 60 percent, according to the Department of Education data. Thousands of*

students have moved into charter schools in districts with both traditional public and charter schools.[15]

The same phenomenon is playing out in the Washington, D.C., suburb of Prince George's County, as the *Washington Post* reports:

> *Adrion Howell has strong connections to the Prince George's County public school system. The 43-year-old lobbyist's mother taught in the schools for 35 years, and Howell attended school there and worked as a substitute teacher in the county before going to Howard University Law School. But, like many other middle-class parents in Prince George's and in urban school districts across the country, when the time came for Howell's daughter, Aaliyah, to attend Glenn Dale Elementary School, he instead enrolled her in a private school.*
>
> *Prince George's has experienced middle-class flight before, when white families departed as the black population grew. But in what is now one of the wealthiest predominantly black counties in the country, more and more affluent black families have turned away from the public schools. Experts say the trend in Prince George's is similar to what has happened in other large school systems that have struggled academically: The loss of middle-class families has led to a higher percentage of poor students using the public school system, less local accountability and waning community involvement.*[16]

A comment on this story on the *Washington Post* website complained about poor discipline and inability to retain good teachers in a chaotic environment. Other commenters chimed in with agreement. Parents are leaving these school districts because they want better educations for their children. And who can blame them? But can these schools be saved? Or should they just be replaced?

*   *   *

HOMESCHOOLING À LA BUFFY

"What about homeschooling? You know, it's not just for scary religious people anymore." That's a line from *Buffy the Vampire Slayer*,[17] and it should strike fear into the hearts, not of vampires, but of public school administrators everywhere.

As noted above, Americans across the country – especially in large, urban (and hence usually subpar) school systems – are increasingly voting with their feet and abandoning traditional public schools, so much so that teachers are increasingly facing layoffs. Some kids are going to charter schools, which are still public but are run more flexibly. Some are leaving for private schools. But many others are going another step beyond traditional education and are switching to online school or even to pure homeschooling.[18] (Hey, it was good enough for Horace Mann's kids.)

And, as Buffy so accurately noted, it's not just "scary religious people." In fact, rather than scary, those religious people are looking more like trendsetters. A recent piece in *The Atlantic* told of purely secular parents' decision to take their kids out of New York City public schools and homeschool instead:

> *That first year, chatting with other homeschooling parents at soccer games, picnics, and after-church coffee hours, I found that our decision was far from unusual. Homeschooling has long been a philosophical choice for religious traditionalists and off-the-grid homesteaders, but for the parents we met – among them several actors, a jazz composer, a restaurateur, a TV chef, a Columbia University physical-plant supervisor, and a handful of college professors – it was a practical alternative to New York's notoriously inadequate education system.*[19]

New York's public school system is indeed notoriously inadequate. And, like most public school systems (or public systems of any kind), it's run more for the convenience of the staff and bureaucrats than for the benefit of parents or kids. Some kids do fine anyway, of course, and some parents aren't in a position to pursue alternatives. But for many parents, traditional schooling is no longer the automatic default choice.

That makes sense. Traditional public schools haven't changed much for decades – and to the extent they have, they've mostly gotten worse. But the rest of the world has changed a lot. The public who eagerly purchased Henry Ford's Model T (available in any color you want, so long as it's black!) now lives in a world in which almost everything is infinitely customized and customizable. That makes one-size-fits-all education, run on a Fordist model, look like a bad deal.

For "notoriously inadequate" public school systems, the risk is that the outflow of kids will turn from a trickle into a flood. At some point, it's a death spiral. As kids (often the best students) leave because schools are "notoriously inadequate," the schools become even more notoriously inadequate, and funding – which is computed on a per-pupil basis – dries up. This, of course, encourages more parents to move their kids elsewhere, in a vicious cycle.

Does this mean the end of public education? No. But it means that the old model – which dates to the 19th century, when schools were explicitly compared to factories – is at risk. Smarter educators will start thinking about how to update a 19th century product to suit 21st century realities. Less-smart educators will hunker down and fight change tooth and nail.

Who will win out in the end? Well, how many 19th century business models do you see flourishing, here in the 21st?

But the consequences for the districts can be devastating. Perhaps worst of all (from public schools' perspective), parents – that is, taxpayers – who are sending their kids elsewhere (especially those who are homeschooling or sending their kids to private or online schools) will probably be less willing to support taxes for the benefit of public schools they're not using and probably don't think highly of. And, for that matter, once public schools are no longer seen as a near universal institution, taxpayer support in general is likely to fall off. That, of course, means schools will be less funded, which will probably encourage still more students to depart and cause more parents to resent paying taxes for public schools their kids don't use, in a vicious circle that produces shrinkage year after year.

At the moment, it's not too late to change public schools for the better. But that window will soon close, as the reputational hit they've taken over the past couple of decades continues to sink in. If that happens – and every force in the system, from administrators to teachers unions to the politicians who depend on their votes, is in favor of the status quo – then we'll see increasing numbers of parents voting with their feet, and a true K-12 implosion will set in.

Some people are more optimistic than others. While visiting Stanford University's Hoover Institution, I spoke with a couple of their experts on educational reform and got two different takes. Terry M. Moe, a professor of political science at Stanford and a senior fellow at Hoover, is gloomy about change from within. The essence of the American political system, he argues, is checks and balances – and those checks and balances make it easy for people to block change. With too many established interests vested in the status quo, political change is pretty much hopeless, he says. Instead, change will come because of technology. Educational technology, via things like online schools and the Khan Academy, is making big waves. And because it's often both much cheaper and better – and because Americans love technology and politicians oppose it at their peril – this technological revolution will overturn things from without.

Eric Hanushek, a senior fellow in education at the Hoover Institution, was more hopeful about political reform. In a recent book, *Schoolhouses, Courthouses, and Statehouses: Solving the Funding-Achievement Puzzle in America's Public Schools*, he outlines ways in which school financing can promote reform. He thinks pressure from parents, and the threat of competition, may be enough to drive change. Teachers unions are a powerful voting bloc, but they're outnumbered by parents.

Both Moe and Hanushek also noted – as did several other people I spoke with in Palo Alto – the strong interest in new education platforms by a variety of startups. Many of these are focusing on college and graduate study, but others are working on K-12 education, and some of the approaches blur the line between the two. And with this degree of interest by startups, we're likely to see more ferment in the future.

It seems clear, at any rate, that things can't go on as they have. Something that can't go on forever, won't, and we can't go on pumping more and more money into education while getting the same (or less) out – especially at a time when parents are increasingly worried about their kids' futures.

Even the author of the *Atlantic* homeschooling article thinks we're heading for rapid change – at both the higher and lower education levels.

One question we're always asked: What about the future? Middle school? High school? The simple answer, for us and plenty of other New York homeschoolers, is that we just don't know; the practicalities change from year to year. Our older boys are now in the fifth grade. They know their way around the Museum of Natural History and Yankee Stadium; they are versed in the exploits of Huck Finn and Jack Sparrow. This spring, they'll take the required state Regents exams – the tests that determine New York City students' options for middle school. But they, and we, hope to continue homeschooling. Meanwhile, when they sit down at the table with protractors or head to a museum, it is college I am thinking about. Not just because a university education is our unquestioned aspiration for our children, but also because it seems to be the closest model for the education we are now trying to provide. Tightly focused class sessions; expert presentations complemented by individual instruction; hands-on learning in areas that vary from day to day and year to year; education undertaken in the wider world – these aspects of our so-called homes- chooling are basic to postsecondary learning. Higher education in America may be very different by 2022, when our twin sons would enroll, but I like to think that they will have had a taste of the university already.[20]

Maybe "lower" education needs to look more like the best parts of higher education. At the very least, it needs to look different. So what's next?

THE NEW PUBLIC EDUCATION

The truth is that nobody knows exactly what comes next. And that may be because nothing in particular is coming. That is, instead of replacing our current monolithic public education system with something equally monolithic, we may wind up replacing our current system with a whole lot of different things, a variety of approaches tailored to chil- dren's (and parents') needs, wants, and pocketbooks. That may not be so bad.

One fast-growing area is online education. Already, more than 1.8 million K-12 students are enrolled in online schools, most of them in high school.[21] Online school – at least for those students with self-discipline – can be far more efficient than a brick-and-mortar school, and that efficiency opens up other opportunities for learning.

My daughter did most of her high school online, after spending one day in ninth grade keeping track of how the public high school she attended spent her time. At the end of eight hours in school, she concluded, she had spent about 2½ hours on actual learning. The rest was absorbed by things like DARE lectures, pep rallies, and other nonacademic activities. Instead, she enrolled in Kaplan's online college-prep program, where she was able to take a lot of Advanced Placement classes not offered in her local public school and where the quality of instruction was higher overall. (In the public school, she reported, her science classes spent a lot of time on the personal difficulties the scientists had had to overcome; at Kaplan, the focus was on their great experiments and why they were important.)

The flexibility also allowed her to work three days a week for a local TV-production company, where she got experience researching and writing for programs shown on the Biography Channel, A&E, etc., something she couldn't have done had she been nailed down in a traditional school. And she still managed to graduate a year early, at age 16, to head off to a "public Ivy" to study engineering.[22]

Did she miss out on socializing at school? Possibly, but at her job she got to spend more time with talented, hardworking adults, which may have been better. (And, as a friend pointed out, nobody ever got shot or knocked up at online school.)

Is online school for everyone? Absolutely not. Some kids don't have the discipline to sit down at a computer every day and do schoolwork with no one looking over their shoulder. (I'm not sure that I would have at that age.) But for the right kids, the online approach offers benefits that traditional school doesn't.

The Khan Academy follows a different approach, known as the flipped classroom, in which lecture-type materials are viewed online at home, while students work on problem sets and get one-on-one help from teachers in the classroom. That way, the parts of school that aren't interactive and involve just absorbing information can be done when there's no teacher around, leaving the teacher in the classroom free to work directly with students. This approach is currently undergoing in-school testing at several locations, but I spoke with one California ninth-grader whose school is part of the program, and she reported that it's been terrific for her. She'd always found math difficult and scary, but now, she says, it makes sense and is much less frightening.

Some children benefit from a Montessori approach that allows kids to follow their own interests and work at their own pace. Other kids benefit from a more rigidly structured traditional approach. Still others do best with homeschooling, which seems to be enormously beneficial for many kids when their parents are willing and able to invest the effort. (Like I said, it was good enough for Horace Mann's kids. And look at how many homeschoolers win the National Spelling Bee. Also, the homeschooled David Karp recently sold Tumblr to Yahoo for a billion dollars.)[23]

Given that there are so many different kinds of kids and, today, so many different kinds of career paths, it makes sense to allow different approaches. This isn't the industrial age anymore. Why pursue a one-size-fits-all approach in education?

At the moment, we do that because we've always done it that way. This is an odd approach, given that education is sold as the ticket to America's future. If that's true, why be guided by the past?

There are, at any rate, two ways in which things can go forward. On the one hand, these new and innovative approaches can take place within the context of publicly funded education. On the other, they can be embraced by parents who are fleeing what they regard as a failing public system. From the standpoint of public schools, the former approach is infinitely better. If parents are free to choose different approaches according to their situations and their children's needs within the public school context, then those parents (and other taxpayers) will see public education as delivering value for their money. And while parents will remain supporters, the children will continue to keep enrollment numbers for the systems up, keeping the public money flowing as well.

On the other hand, if the only way parents can avail themselves of these new approaches is to exit the public school system, then they are likely to be resentful of the taxes they pay. And if enough people exit the public schools for other environments, taxpayers in general may come to regard public education as, essentially, just another program for the poor. That's likely to mean a steadily decreasing willingness to provide financial support, especially in times when there is competition from other budget priorities.

Which approach will win out? At this point it's hard to say, but here's one indicator: more and more public schools are offering online programs of their own, usually through a national vendor like K12.com. Sometimes these programs are designed to accommodate kids who are physically unable to attend school or who have behavioral problems. But they're also appearing now as genuine alternatives. School systems like it because online education is cheaper, leaving them with more money to spend on other things. And many parents and students like it because of the flexibility.

Flexibility may be a hidden payoff of a more open approach to public education in general. It's easy to miss just how many rigidities are introduced into American life by the traditional public school approach, but those rigidities are legion. Getting rid of them may help address other problems.

Real estate prices, for example, are heavily influenced by the quality of local public schools. Poor people often can't afford to attend top-flight public schools because they can't afford to live in the district. People who own property in those districts, meanwhile, stand to lose a significant amount of their home's value if the school board rezones them into a district with less-favored schools. Often people are forced to live in areas they'd otherwise rather not – because of long commutes, for example – simply in order to avail their kids of a decent education. By cutting the link between location and school quality, those problems could be eliminated, likely resulting in substantial savings for society – and parents.

Kids, too, would get additional flexibility. As I mentioned, one of the great fringe benefits of my daughter's experience with online school was that she was able to hold down a job. She spent 12 hours a week working at a TV-production company, doing work that ranged from the semiglamorous – doing research and writing treatments for shows that aired on Biography and A&E – to the not glamorous at all, like filing videotapes, processing expense reports, and making coffee.

That experience was enormously valuable to her. Few other kids have two years of high-level work experience at the age of 16, and she learned not only specific skills but also the broader talents of working in an office and getting along with people. That was huge, and it's not the kind of thing you learn when cooped up in a building with a bunch of other teenagers. (Perhaps most valuable, she got the experience of sorting the résumés sent in by people applying for jobs. That teaches things that can be learned nowhere else.)

I frequently hear employers complain that entry-level employees, even in their 20s, don't really understand how to operate in a workplace environment; all they've ever known is school, and school is an unnatural environment. A more flexible approach to public education might help address this by allowing more teenagers to get work earlier. Many education reformers have talked about the value of apprenticeship-style models; it's a lot easier to do that sort of thing when you're not stuck listening to DARE lectures all day.

SOME FUTURE SCENARIOS

With the federal government strapped and with many states and municipalities looking at budget cuts and even bankruptcy, spending on K-12 education can't continue increasing at current rates. It particularly can't continue increasing at current rates when the results remain so dismal.

Something that can't go on forever, won't. So these educational trends won't continue indefinitely. What will we see instead? Based on what we know to date, it seems likely that a new solution will be one that is:

1. CHEAPER. Costs are out of control, and taxpayers are out of money. Stopping the runaway increases will be the first priority, but over the mid- to longer term, school

systems will be looking for actual savings. There's no reason, in an age of exploding information technology, that the United States should be spending so much more than other countries to educate its kids.

2. BETTER. Current education isn't just expensive; it's also not very good. Despite high per-student spending, U.S. students lag behind other countries. Much time in school is wasted, and the smarter kids are often held back by classes designed not to leave the slower kids behind. What comes next will have to be better than what we have now. Fortunately, that won't be terribly hard.

3. MORE FLEXIBLE. Accommodating the districts, schedules, and other requirements of public school systems introduces all sorts of costs and distortions into other parts of life: real estate prices, commuting patterns, and the ability of teenagers to seek gainful employment. This one-size-fits-all approach may have made sense 100 years ago, when society was simpler and alternatives were scarce. It doesn't make sense anymore.

4. MORE DIVERSE. Speaking of one size fits all, the old-fashioned approach of treating students like interchangeable parts in an industrial-age machine doesn't fit with the wide variances among students in abilities, learning styles, and interests. Again, 100 years ago it may have made sense to take our square-peg kids and educationally hammer them into societal round holes. Today, not so much. In our more diverse society – and economy – it makes more sense to let kids learn in ways that play to their own particular strengths.

5. MORE PARENT-FRIENDLY. With smaller families the norm and with changing societal attitudes toward parenting, many of today's parents are more involved and interested in their kids' educations. These parents aren't happy just shipping their kids off to an educa-

tional warehouse for the day. They want to know what's going on and to take a hand in directing things.

Given these characteristics, perhaps it makes more sense to speak of *solutions,* rather than *a solution.* Rather than looking for the one best way to educate our kids, we might be better off putting together a diversified portfolio of educational approaches, some of which work better for some kids in some circumstances and some of which work better for other kids in other circumstances. Such an approach is likely to produce better outcomes, and at lower costs.

But given that something that can't go on forever, won't, one thing is certain: change is coming to public education, and in a major way. Educators would be well advised to move with the tide, rather than trying to stand against it.

Some Quasi-Predictions

When you write that the present situation can't hold, everybody wants to know what comes next. If I were sure about that, I'd be starting a company to cash in (I've always kind of fancied owning a private jet) instead of writing a book whose sales are almost certain not to land me in private-jet territory. But while, as noted, I can't predict the future, I can take a hint. Here are some things I think we'll see in education, both at K-12 and higher education levels.

CUSTOMIZATION

At all levels, I think the trend is moving away from old-fashioned models to more variety. We live in a world with thousands of varieties of shampoo; why should we be satisfied with so little real variation in education? If the 19th century was about standardization, the 21st is about customization. If the technology that underlay everything in the 19th century was the steam engine, what should education look like in a century in which the archetypal technology is something more like a 3-D printer? In fact, it wouldn't be surprising to see the distinctions between K-12 and higher education (both, after all, 19th century models) blur or vanish.

I can imagine a future where children are tested at a very early age and then retested repeatedly as they grow up, and where their individualized educational model changes in response to their learning styles, their needs, and their interests (and their parents' interests). This would go far beyond the "achievement tests" and "tracking" used in current schools and might even look something like a video game, in which students' learning is more like play and in which the nature of their performance changes what comes next on an ongoing basis.

GAMIFICATION

In fact, there's a big lesson here. The video-game industry is already a leader in holding young people's interest and getting them to acquire all sorts of arcane skills, at vastly lower cost than the educational system. Much of this is in shoot-'em-up settings, but not all. American troops are already using video games in training. Some are fancy custom jobs, like the combat simulators described in this article by James Dunnigan at StrategyPage:

> [The simulators] *surround the trainees and replicate the sights and sounds of an attack. Weapons equipped with special sensors allow the troops to shoot back from mockups of vehicles, and they also receive feedback if they are hit.... One problem with the ambushes and roadside bombs is that not every soldier driving around Iraq will encounter one, but if you do, your chances of survival go up enormously if you quickly make the right moves. The troops know this.*[1]

The Army has also developed a game called *America's Army,* originally intended as a recruiting tool, but which has turned out to be realistic enough that it's used by the military for training purposes.[2] These training games draw heavily on existing technology, most of it developed for consumer-market video games. (And, in fact, the military uses some consumer games in training too.) They also draw on troops' skills at rapidly mastering such simulators, skills likely honed on consumer video games.

But the skills that games can teach go well beyond the military, as I discovered some years ago firsthand when I heard my daughter and one of her friends having an earnest discussion: "You have to have a job to buy food and things, and if you don't go to work, you get fired. And if you spend all your money buying stuff, you have to make more."

All true enough, and advice worthy of Clark Howard or Dave Ramsey. And it's certainly something my daughter had heard from me over the years. But rather than quoting paternal wisdom, they were talking about *The Sims,* a computer game that simulates ordinary American life, which swept through my patch of Little-Girl Land at breakneck speed some time ago. Thanks to *The Sims,* the girls learned how to make a budget and how to read an income statement – and to be worried when the cash flow goes negative. They learned about comparison shopping. They also picked up some pointers on human interaction, though *The Sims* characters come up short in that department. (Then again, so do real people, now and then, but the *Sims* characters can have affairs, and when they do, they usually end badly. In *Sims* world, as in real life, the bourgeois virtues generally pay off.)

A later version, *The Sims 2,* upped the stakes. Among other things, as its label makes clear, it allows players to "Mix Genes: Your Sims have DNA and inherit physical and personality traits. Take your Sims through an infinite number of generations as you evolve their family tree." What more could a father want than a game that will teach his daughter that if you marry a loser, he'll likely stay a loser, and if you have kids with him, they'll have a good chance of being losers too? Thank God for technology.

My daughter is well past the little-girl stage now, but I do think she acquired useful knowledge and skills from all the hours she spent playing *The Sims.* She's certainly excellent with money, and so far she's avoided losers in her budding romantic life. So three cheers for *The Sims.* Most video games are more about escapism than teaching, I suspect, but that could change – there's no reason why more sophisticated versions of *The Sims*, now available in *The Sims 3, The Sims Medieval,* and various other iterations – could do a lot of the teaching. As technology advances and immersive technology improves, I can imagine a lot of very useful teaching working this way. And with the addition of immersive technology that can go out into the real world – more advanced versions of Google Glass – a lot of things can be taught in a very different fashion. Perhaps, overlaid on your field of vision will be instructions on fixing an engine, with the appropriate parts highlighted and with pop-up instructions on what to do next.

Video-game companies are better at holding young people's attention in an interactive fashion than anyone else. Expect more here.

INTEGRATION

Traditionally, education was a precursor to, well, actually living. You spent years in school, then you emerged into the real world, leaving pencils and books behind. In the old days, that worked pretty well: things changed slowly enough that what you could learn in college, or even in high school, was all you'd need for a lifetime. In the few areas where that wasn't true, we had specialized graduate degrees like the PhD or the JD, which were supposed to assure that their holders not only knew things but also knew how to teach themselves whatever else they needed to know later.

Nowadays, though, that's pretty much everyone. The solution is not to send everyone for a PhD or JD, though. Instead, the wall separating school and life needs to be broken down. This has consequences reaching in both directions. On the one hand, people may leave school for the real world sooner; if you're going to have to keep learning all the way along, there's no point trying to cram *everything* into your head in advance. On the other hand, just because you're out of school won't mean an end to learning. My exhaustive study of WordPerfect 4.2 did not, sadly, mean an end to learning word-processing programs, and that phenomenon is likely to apply to many, many more areas, not solely involving technology.

Already, a growing percentage of higher-ed enrollees are older "re-entry" students. Some of these are people going to college for the first time at 40; others are people seeking additional education in areas they need to know. Traditional college settings don't serve them particularly well, which has been one of the reasons behind the growth of online (often but not always for-profit) educational institutions. We'll see more movement in that direction, but we'll also probably see more effort earlier in the education process to give people more self-teaching skills. At least we should. Resilience pays, especially in a world where things are changing fast.

CHEAPIFICATION

Driving everything in this book, of course, is the notion that education at all levels is just too expensive. Like many other knowledge industries, I expect information technology to drive costs, and prices, down significantly. (We may even see university administration outsourced to low-paid part-timers the way teaching has been. Hey, it could happen.) This change won't be so great for the producers – plummeting prices seldom are – but it will be a huge boon for the con-sumers. When things become cheaper, consumers consume more of them. If more people consume more education, we'll have a more educated populace. That's a good thing, right?

*　*　*

FRAGMENTATION

One of the things that Horace Mann sought from the Prussians in compulsory public education was a sort of centripetal institution – something that would promote a shared sense of citizenship and nationhood. Is this an unalloyed good? Maybe, maybe not. We might be better, at least, if the Germans had stayed a bit less unified (and so, for that matter, might be the Germans). On the other hand, it's possible that the unifying force of assimilative public education allowed the United States to take in huge numbers of immigrants in the 19th and early 20th centuries while maintaining social cohesion. That's something to bear in mind as we talk about increased immigration in the 21st century – though on the other hand, it seems to me that the people running public education today are much less enthusiastic about assimilation than the people running public education were a century ago. Just because public education *can* foster assimilation doesn't mean that it has to.

TRANSFORMATION?

Beyond the scope of this book, of course, is the larger question of whether automation and machine intelligence will make computers and robots better at doing almost every job than humans. Some find this a troubling possibility. I once asked one of my law, science, and technology seminars to imagine jobs that would survive the appearance of robots and cheap artificial intelligence. The class consensus was that the best chances for job survival were for massage therapists, prostitutes, and – in light of LegalZoom, I think they were being a bit hopeful here – lawyers. But if robots wind up doing everything else, they noted, it might be hard to earn the money to *pay* the prostitutes and massage therapists. And there's already talk of sexbots[3] or, as science-fiction writer Greg Bear amusingly calls them, "prosthetutes." So what's left?

Futurists like Ray Kurzweil doubt that this problem will present itself, because they see human enhancement – essentially, computer-brain interfaces – as making humans at least as competent as the robots and ultimately blurring the distinctions between human and robot work. I suppose that counts as a sort of "education," too, but one that is, as I say, beyond the scope of this book.

What seems clear, though, is that the transition to a world run by robots and AI is barely beginning, and people have to earn a living in the meantime. With the world changing faster, it is a good thing that education is likely to become much cheaper, and more adaptable, along the way.

Some Concluding Thoughts

My University of Tennessee colleague Ben Barton has a book in the works – on the future of the legal profession and of legal education – that in some interesting ways parallels this one. When I got to his surprisingly sunny concluding chapter, I sent him this passage from Arthur Allen Leff as a cautionary note:

> *The radically unknown is always frightening (at least to those making out all right as is), especially considering how many lives can be lashed to pieces as a new distributional curve flails about, desperately seeking a new equilibrium.*[1]

Massive change, even change that is, overall, for the better, leaves a lot of wreckage behind. Schumpeter's "creative destruction" is creative, but it is also destructive, and the benefits and detriments of change are not evenly distributed. Many win, but there are losers too.

So who will win and who will lose as a result of the sweeping changes that are likely to come in both higher and lower education? As usual, when technology advances and markets open, consumers will win, while the most comfortable among the producers will find their lives, at best, less comfortable.

For a long time, the providers of education at all levels have enjoyed a sort of guildlike monopoly. And as economist

John Hicks notes, as quoted earlier, "The best of all monopoly profits is a quiet life."[2] Alas, the lives of education providers are likely to be less quiet and comfortable than they have been. When education was in the hands of guilds made up of educators, as it has largely been for over a century, educators unsurprisingly took advantage of their control to arrange things to their liking. That will change significantly in the years to come.

Neither higher education nor K-12 schooling will remain in the hands of the guilds in the future, though we can expect a significant rear-guard action on their part. But the vulnerability they face is that it will become easier and easier for people to avoid the guilds entirely thanks to the new alternatives that technology (and other changes – but mostly technology) has made possible.

For consumers – that is, students and parents – this is a big improvement. We take it for granted that people have to spend a minimum of 17 years (13 in K-12 and four in college) and often significantly longer getting themselves ready to enter the real world. But doing so is extremely expensive. The financial costs of schooling, at all levels, are outrageous, and as we have seen, those costs have been growing at an unsustainable pace. And the financial costs are not the only ones involved. Seventeen years (and that is an optimistic timeline) is a long time to spend on the bench instead of playing the game. If you graduate at 22 and work until 70, you'll have a working life of 48 years, meaning that you will have spent *over a third* of that time in school getting ready. "Ask me for anything but time," Napoleon famously told his generals. But our system asks for a lot of time indeed.

There are spiritual costs too. For some – disproportionately, I suspect, those who go on to become educators, or writers about education – school is actually pleasant. They are good at it, they are rewarded and recognized for their ability, and it seems easier than the real world.[3] But for many others, it is crushingly dull – an experience captured in the Eagles' song about high school, "Teenage Jail" – and, other than as a credential, not particularly useful in the years to come. Time that could have been spent on something creative, or at least satisfying – meaningful work, even if it's folding shirts at a men's store – is spent on things that have no meaning in themselves. As we've seen, for many students the best years of their lives, years in which they might have been accomplishing things or learning responsibility, are spent in settings in which responsibility is scarce and accomplishments are mostly make-believe.

Dan Pink – in his recent book on career satisfaction and ambition, *Drive* – reports that modern research identifies three key areas of job satisfaction: mastery, autonomy, and purpose.[4] Mastery refers not to a complete knowledge of a job but rather to a job that poses continuous challenges that draw on one's deep skills; autonomy refers to a degree of control over what one does and how one does it; and purpose has to do with feeling like part of a group working toward a common goal. If these are key elements to job satisfaction, is it wrong to think that they might also play a role in how people experience education? Even when they're not teenage jails, most contemporary educational institutions don't rate very well on this scale.

And though some degree of education is essential, we've also seen that the evidence that college reduces income inequality is skimpy, with some research suggesting quite the opposite. (Even *New York Times* columnist Paul Krugman has admitted, "Education, then, is no longer the answer to rising inequality, if it ever was.")[5] Add to this the massive cost – reflected in student-loan debt, long time-to-graduation, or depletion of parental assets that may be needed for retirement – and the argument for college as some sort of generic earnings enhancer seems pretty weak. For some graduates, it will enhance earnings. For others it will not. And many who invest a lot of time and money will never graduate at all.

For these people the current system isn't working. If it is replaced – as I think likely – by a system that is faster, cheaper, and more focused on delivering what students need, they will be much better off than they are now. Instead of entering the adult world at 22, or 25, they will be able to work and earn and direct their own lives at 18, or 20, and without the burden of student debt faced by so many young adults now. Perhaps later in life they'll re-enter the educational world to learn something different, but they won't be postponing adulthood to do it. A cheaper and more flexible educational system will make such later-life education (involving more, I think, than just "retraining") much easier.

The losers, on the other hand will be, well, people like me: tenured academics or unionized K-12 teachers, those who, in Leff's words, are making out all right as it is. The comfortable life that the previous arrangement's quasi-monopoly profits permitted will, most likely, grow less comfortable. There will probably be higher teaching loads, less classroom autonomy, and, over time, lower pay for most.

In fact, we're already seeing this to a degree in higher education. While life remains sweet for tenured academics – and nearly as sweet for those on the tenure track – more and more of the actual university teaching being done is performed by adjuncts and lecturers who are not on the tenure track, work year to year (or sometimes semester to semester) without job security, and face high teaching loads for low pay (often without benefits) with no support or time off for research. The model is much like what happened in declining unionized industries in manufacturing: senior employees managed to hold onto a pretty good deal as their numbers gradually shrank, while new hires came in under much less favorable terms.

For the low-paid adjuncts, though, the new approaches may generate better jobs, better pay (that won't be hard), and more opportunity to advance than being at the bottom of the prestige totem pole at a traditional university. If today's tenured academics are, as someone suggested to me once, the closest thing you can get in the modern world to being minor nobility, then today's adjuncts and lecturers are more like serfs toiling in the academic fields. The changes we're experiencing are not likely to convert serfs into barons, but they may at least gain more freedom, more respect, and somewhat more money in a postfeudal academic world.

Transitions are usually painful, though. As noted earlier, white-collar workers who watched blue-collar jobs disappear in the 1980s and 1990s felt the pain only secondhand – until their jobs started to disappear too. For the educators at all levels whose jobs disappear or become less pleasant, the pain will be real, as life plans collapse and benefits constrict. But, of course, the pain suffered by students – in the form of indebtedness, lost opportunities, and wasted years – was also experienced by those educators, if at all, only secondhand. The educational future is thus one that, post-transition, is likely to be brighter for consumers, if somewhat less rosy for the most comfortable producers. In this, it resembles many other areas of the economy.

Even for the consumers, of course, the transitional period may be rough and confusing. For the producers – teachers, professors, and the rest – things may be worse as, in Leff's words, the "distributional curve flails about, desperately seeking a new equilibrium." But comfortable or not, change is coming. Those who face it are likely to do better than those who refuse to.

AFTERWORD

Everybody knows there's a problem, even if some people are still in denial. In fact, when I started writing about this subject, I told my dean that I was surprised I hadn't gotten more flak. His response: Everybody knows there's a problem; they just don't want to talk about it because they don't know what to do about it, and they're afraid of what they might have to do if they did.

I think that's right. For the past decade or so, and especially since the economic downturn in 2008, I've seen a lot of academics privately express a queasy discomfort with how we operate, with the burdens it imposes on students (especially in the form of debt), and with whether, ultimately, it's sustainable. Some of those conversations reminded me of conversations I had with journalists at traditional-media newspapers and magazines a decade earlier: a frank admission that the system can't go on as it is coupled with a sheepish hope that it will nonetheless somehow continue to do so until the speaker reaches retirement age.

Some of those journalists have since been laid off. Others are worried about it, while still others took their buyouts and tried something new, for better or worse. (Usually, as it turns out, for better.) The old business model for newspapers and magazines, which was riding high in the 1980s and 1990s, doesn't work so well now.

I can't help but feel that what's happened to journalists is in the process of happening to academics too. The academic world, by design, changes much more slowly than the world of media, but we are a knowledge industry too and are no more likely, in the long run, to flourish by sticking to a 19th century model in the second decade of the 21st. Pointing this out sometimes upsets people who would rather not think about it, but I am no more rooting for disaster than someone who is on the deck of the *Titanic* saying, "Hey, I think I see an iceberg out there."

I don't think the changes coming in education are as destructive as the *Titanic*'s sinking – though for some involved, it may seem that way. Indeed, as I've noted, I expect that for the consumers of education, they are likely to be largely beneficial. But I do think that, beneficial or not, substantial changes are inevitable. It is past time to think about how to make those changes as rewarding as possible for everyone.

NOTES

IN THE BEGINNING

1 For a discussion of this phenomenon generally, see Glenn Harlan Reynolds, *An Army of Davids* (2006), 1–10.

2. Robert William Fogel, *The Escape from Hunger and Premature Death: 1700–2100* (2004).

3 Fogel, 2.

4 Adam Smith, *An Inquiry into the Nature and Causes of the Wealth of Nations* (Modern Library, 1937), 4–5.

5 Paul E. Peterson, *Saving Schools* (2010), 25.

6 Peterson, *Saving Schools*, 27.

7 William Clark, *Academic Charisma and the Origins of the Research University* (2008), 12–14.

8 See Bob Pepperman Taylor, *Horace Mann's Troubling Legacy: The Education of Democratic Citizens,* 38–46, 69–70. For the cast-iron/wax quote, see 30. See also William Hayes, *Horace Mann's Vision of the Public Schools: Is It Still Relevant?* (2006), 20–28.

9 Peterson, *Saving Schools*, 30.

10 Derek Bok, *Our Underachieving Colleges* (2006), 14.

11 Clark, *Academic Charisma*, 16. "The German university was a professorial university; the English was a collegiate university in which professors played a marginal role until the twentieth century."

12 John Walz, *German Influence in American Education and Culture* (1936), 53. See also Laurence Veysey, *The Emergence of the American University* (1965), 125–179.

13 For a concise history, see Daniel Fallon, "German Influences on American Education," in *The German-American Encounter: Conflict and Cooperation Between Two Cultures, 1800–2000,* ed. Frank Trommler and Elliott Shore (2001), 77–87. See also Roger L. Geiger, *To Advance Knowledge: The Growth of American Research Universities* (1986), 7–8. ("The mission of research in American universities has been irrevocably associated with the founding of the Johns Hopkins University in 1876: 'Perhaps the single most decisive event in the history of learning in the Western hemisphere,' as it has been extravagantly, but not unreasonably, described.")

14 Geiger, 8.

15 Geiger, 11.

16 *Id.*

17 Clark, *Academic Charisma,* 13. "The wise minister manages academics through their vanity."

HIGHER EDUCATION

1 Penelope Wang, "Is College Still Worth the Price?" *Money,* April 13, 2009, http://money.cnn.com/2008/08/20/pf/college/college_price. moneymag/.

2 Ron Lieber, "Placing the Blame as Students Are Buried in Debt," *New York Times,* May 29, 2010, http://www.nytimes.com/2010/05/29/ your-money/student-loans/29money.html?_r=0.

3 David Segal, "High Debt and Falling Demand Trap New Vets," *New York Times,* February 24, 2013, http://www.nytimes.com/2013/02/24/ business/high-debt-and-falling-demand-trap-new-veterinarians. html?pagewanted=all&_r=2&.

4 Jenna Johnson, "At Occupy Wall Street Protests, Student Loan Frustration," *Washington Post,* October 10, 2011, http://www.washington-post.com/blogs/campus-overload/post/ at-occupy-wall-street-protests-student-loan-frustration/2011/10/10/ gIQAV5CHaL_blog.html.

5 Kenneth Anderson, "The Fragmenting of New Class Elites, or, Downward Mobility," The Volokh Conspiracy, October 31, 2011, http:// www.volokh.com/2011/10/31/the-fragmenting-of-the-new-class-elites-or-downward-mobility/.

6 Richard Vedder, "There Are as Many Student Loan Debtors as College Graduates," *Chronicle of Higher Education,* April 11, 2012, http:// chronicle.com/blogs/innovations/ there-are-as-many-student-loan-debtors-as-college-graduates/31944.

7 Janet Lorin, "Student Loan Debt Reaches Record $1 Trillion, Report Says," *Bloomberg News,* March 22, 2012, http://www.bloomberg.com/ news/2012-03-22/student-loan-debt-reaches-record-1-trillion-u-s-re-port-says.html.

8 Al Yoon, "Investors Say No to Sallie Mae Bond Deal: Poor Demand for Security Backed Only by Excess Cash Flow Shows Limits to Appetite for Risk," *Wall Street Journal,* April 26, 2013, online.wsj.com/ article/SB10001424127887323335404578444832431703020.html.

In the case of the canceled Sallie Mae offering, rising defaults could have crimped the cash flow of the federally backed loans supporting the new securities, because more defaults would mean less excess, or residual, income after holders of the original loans were paid.

What's more, regulators and lawmakers have become concerned about growing levels of student debt, raising the risk political decisions could alter the bond market for student loans, said Jeffrey Klingelhofer, a portfolio manager at Thornburg Investment Management. For instance, a program that would allow borrowers to refinance their loans would reduce cash flow, Mr. Klingelhofer said.

9   John Carney, "The Student Loan Bubble Is Starting to Burst," CNBC, September 5, 2013, http://www.cnbc.com/id/101012270.

10 Annie Lowrey, "Student Debt Slows Growth as Young Spend Less," *New York Times,* May 11, 2013, http://www.nytimes.com/2013/05/11/business/economy/student-loan-debt-weighing-down-younger-us-workers.html.

11 "Young Student Loan Borrowers Retreat From Housing and Auto Markets," Federal Reserve Bank of New York, April 17, 2013, http://libertystreeteconomics.newyorkfed.org/2013/04/young-student-loan-borrowers-retreat-from-housing-and-auto-markets.html.

12 "Decline in LSAT Test-Takers Portends 'Death Spiral' for Low-Ranked Law Schools," TaxProf, March 20, 2012, http://taxprof.typepad.com/taxprof_blog/2012/03/decline-in-.html

13 Reuben Fischer-Baum, "Is Your State's Highest-Paid Employee a Coach? (Probably)," Deadspin, May 9, 2013, http://deadspin.com/infographic-is-your-states-highest-paid-employee-a-co-489635228. In most states, it's a football or basketball coach; in New Hampshire, it's a hockey coach; in the rest, it's university presidents or law- and medical-school deans.

14 John Quinterno and Viany Orozco, "The Great Cost Shift: How Higher Education Cuts Undermine the Future Middle Class," Demos, April 3, 2012, http://www.demos.org/publication/great-cost-shift-how-higher-education-cuts-undermine-future-middle-class

15 Ry Rivard, "Downgrading Elite Colleges," Inside Higher Ed, August 30,2013,http://www.insidehighered.com/news/2013/08/30/prestigious-liberal-arts-colleges-face-ratings-downgrades. ("Over the past year and a half, the credit ratings of several prestigious liberal arts colleges have been downgraded or assigned a negative outlook by Moody's Investors Service. These are institutions – Haverford College, Morehouse College, Oberlin College and Wellesley College – that top students seek out, yet they are showing small but noticeable signs of fiscal stress several years after the end of the recession. Their downgraded ratings are still better than those of plenty of other institutions, and Moody's has issued plenty of gloomy projects about colleges during the economic downturn. But the recent actions are notable because they affect colleges that are by many measures – money, prestige, history – among the most fortunate in the country.")

16 Heather Mac Donald, "Less Academics, More Narcissism," *City Journal,* July 14, 2011, http://www.city-journal.org/2011/cjc0714hm.html.

17 Mike Adams, "My New Diversity Merger Proposal," Townhall.com, October 26, 2011, http://townhall.com/columnists/mikeadams/2011/10/26/my_new_diversity_merger_proposal/page/full/.

18 Scott Jaschik, "Backwards on Racial Understanding," Inside Higher Ed, April 10, 2012, http://www.insidehighered.com/news/2012/04/10/study-suggests-students-grow-less-interested-promoting-racial-understanding.

19 Heather Mac Donald, "Multiculti U.," *City Journal,* Spring 2013, http://www.city-journal.org/2013/23_2_multiculti-university.html.

20 Michael Barone, "Will College Bubble Burst From Public Subsidies?" *Washington Examiner,* March 19, 2012, http://washingtonexaminer.com/article/116377. ("Take the California State University system, the second tier in that state's public higher education. Between 1975 and 2008 the number of faculty rose by 3 percent, to 12,019 positions. During those same years the number of administrators rose 221 percent, to 12,183. That's right: There are more administrators than teachers at Cal State now. These people get paid to 'liaise' and 'facilitate' and produce reports on diversity. How that benefits Cal State students or California taxpayers is unclear.")

21 Mark J. Perry, "Michigan: 53% More Administrators Than Faculty," Carpe Diem, July 25, 2011, http://mjperry.blogspot.com/2011/07/univ-of-michigan-53-more-administrators.html.

22 Benjamin Ginsberg, "Administrators Ate My Tuition," *Washington Monthly,* September/October 2011, http://www.washingtonmonthly.com/magazine/septemberoctober_2011/features/administrators_ate_my_tuition031641.php.

23 For more on the explosion of educational administrators, see Benjamin Ginsberg's book-length treatment, *The Fall of the Faculty: The Rise of the All-Administrative University and Why It Matters* (2011). Here's a bit on administrators and meetings:

> *The number of administrators and staffers on university campuses has increased so rapidly in recent years that often there is simply not enough work to keep them busy.... I am always struck by the fact that so many well-paid individuals have so little to do. To fill their time, administrators engage in a number of make-work activities. They attend meetings and conferences, they organize and attend administrative and staff retreats, and they participate in the strategic planning processes that have become commonplace on many campuses. While these activities are time consuming, their actual contribution to the core research and*

teaching missions of the university is questionable. Little would be lost if all pending administrative retreats and conferences, as well as four of every five staff meetings (these could be selected at random) were canceled tomorrow.

    Id., 41. Based on my own experience at universities, I have to agree with this assessment.

24 Ruth Simon, "Colleges Cut Prices by Providing More Financial Aid," *Wall Street Journal,* May 6, 2013, http://online.wsj.com/article/SB100 01424127887324582004578461450531723268.html.

25 Eric Kelderman, "Ashland University Slashes Tuition," *Chronicle of Higher Education,* August 28, 2013, http://chronicle.com/blogs/ bottomline/ashland-u-slashes-tuition-by-37/.

26 *Id.*

27 Paul L. Caron, "Law School Applications, Starting Salaries (but Not Tuition) Sink to Pre-1985 Levels," TaxProf, January 16, 2013, http:// taxprof.typepad.com/taxprof_blog/2013/01/merritt-.html.

28 Paul L. Caron, "There Are Two Law School Grads for Every Law Job," TaxProf, May 15, 2013, http://taxprof.typepad.com/taxprof_blog/ 2013/05/american-lawyer-.html.

29 Ethan Bronner, "Law Schools' Applications Fall as Costs Rise and Jobs Are Cut," *New York Times,* January 31, 2013, http://www.nytimes. com/2013/01/31/education/law-schools-applications-fall-as-costs-rise-and-jobs-are-cut.html?smid=pl-share&_r=1&.

30 *Id.*

31 *Id.*

32 *Id.*

33 Paul L. Caron, "Kansas to Shrink Entering 1L Class By 30%," Tax-Prof, May 28, 2013, http://taxprof.typepad.com/taxprof_blog/2013/ 05/kansas-to-shrink.html.

34 For an in-depth discussion of legal education's business-model problems, see Brian Z. Tamanaha, *Failing Law Schools* (2012).

35 See, e.g., Jon Wolper, "Vermont Law School Gives Buyouts to 10 Workers," *Valley News,* January 18, 2013, http://www.vnews.com/news/ 3896880-95/buyouts-laid-law-members.

36 Paul L. Caron, "Catholic University Imposes 20% Budget Cut Due to Declining Law School Enrollment," TaxProf, April 17, 2013, http:// taxprof.typepad.com/taxprof_blog/2013/04/catholic.html.

    The law school accounts for about 10% of the university's overall enrollment, so the mind reels at the extent to which the rest of the university has been depending for its solvency on encouraging the law school to produce massively indebted graduates who are unable to get any sort of legal job in what is at present the worst place in

the country to try to get a job as a lawyer (Washington DC).
This naturally raises the question of how many other universi-
ties depend on their law school's graduates to cross-subsidize the
rest of the campus to a similar extent.

37 Neil Shah, "Smaller Share of High School Grads Going to College," *Wall Street Journal,* April 17, 2013, http://blogs.wsj.com/economics/2013/04/17/smaller-share-of-high-school-grads-going-to-college/.

38 Catherine Rampell, "It Takes a B.A. to Find a Job as a File Clerk," *New York Times,* February 20, 2013, http://www.nytimes.com/2013/02/20/business/college-degree-required-by-increasing-number-of-companies.html?hp&_r=3&.

39 *Id.*

40 Carol Morello, "More College-Educated Jump Tracks to Become Skilled Manual Laborers," *Washington Post,* June 15, 2010, http://www.washingtonpost.com/wp-dyn/content/article/2010/06/14/AR2010061402838.html.

41 *Id.*

42 Don Lee, "Is a College Degree Still Worth It?" *Los Angeles Times,* June 12, 2010, http://web.archive.org/web/20100706223324/http://www.latimes.com/business/la-fi-jobs-educate-20100612,0,5466021,full.story. ("The Bureau of Labor Statistics projects that seven of the 10 employment sectors that will see the largest gains over the next decade won't require much more than some on-the-job training. These include home healthcare aides, customer service representatives and food preparers and servers. Meanwhile, well-paying white-collar jobs such as computer programming have become vulnerable to outsourcing to foreign countries. 'People with bachelor's degrees will increasingly get not very highly satisfactory jobs,' said W. Norton Grubb, a professor at UC Berkeley's School of Education. 'In that sense, people are getting more schooling than jobs are available.'")

43 Steve Earle, "Hillbilly Highway," http://www.metrolyrics.com/hillbilly-highway-lyrics-steve-earle.html

Now he worked and saved his money
So that one day he might send
My old man off to college
To use his brains and not his hands

But contrast Earle's world – in which his dad wound up with "a good job in Houston" – with this view of the near future from science fiction writer Neal Stephenson:

When it gets down to it – we're talking trade balances here – once
we've brain-drained all our technology into other countries, once

things have evened out, they're making cars in Bolivia and micro-
waves in Tadzhikistan and selling them here – once our edge in
natural resources has been made irrelevant by giant Hong Kong
ships and dirigibles that can ship North Dakota all the way to
New Zealand for a nickel – once the Invisible Hand has taken all
those historical inequities and smeared them out into a broad
global layer of what a Pakistani bricklayer would consider to be
prosperity – y'know what? There's only four things we do better
than anyone else:

music
movies
microcode (software)
high-speed pizza delivery.

Neal Stephenson, *Snow Crash* (2000). In Stephenson's near future, proximity is an advantage.

44 Kevin Kiley, "The Other Debt Crisis," Inside Higher Ed, April 10, 2012, http://www.insidehighered.com/news/2012/04/10/public-universities-will-take-more-debt-states-decrease-spending-capital-projects.

45 Scott Jaschik, "Study Finds Large Numbers of College Students Don't Learn Much," Inside Higher Ed, January 18, 2011, http://www.insidehighered.com/news/2011/01/18/study_finds_large_numbers_of_college_students_don_t_learn_much#ixzz1rJJkvqqR.

46 Andrew S. Rosen, *Change.edu: Rebooting for the New Talent Economy* (2011), 133–135.

47 Andrew Ferguson, *Crazy U: One Dad's Crash Course in Getting His Kid Into College* (2011), 63.

48 Ferguson, 9.

49 See Elizabeth A. Armstrong and Laura Hamilton, *Paying for the Party: How College Maintains Inequality* (2013), 216–219.

50 *Id.*

51 Armstrong and Hamilton, 209.

52 Richard Arum and Josipa Roksa, *Academically Adrift: Limited Learning on College Campuses* (2011), 53–54.

53 Arum and Roksa, 54.

54 *Id.*

55 Elizabeth Dwoskin, "Will You Marry Me (After I Pay Off My Student Loans)?" *Businessweek,* March 28, 2012, http://www.businessweek.com/articles/2012-03-28/will-you-marry-me-after-i-pay-off-my-student-loans.

56 http://ocw.mit.edu.

57 http://www.wgu.edu.

58 Jordan Weissmann, "Can This 'Online Ivy' University Change the

Face of Higher Education?" *The Atlantic,* April 5, 2012, http://www.theatlantic.com/business/archive/2012/04/can-this-online-ivy-university-change-the-face-of-higher-education/255471/.

59 "In Blurring of Online Courses, Traditional Georgia Tech to Offer Full Open Online Master's,"Associated Press, May 15, 2013, http://news.yahoo.com/georgia-tech-offer-full-online-000208782.html.

60 Andy Kessler, "Professors Are About to Get an Online Education: Georgia Tech's New Internet Master's Degree in Computer Science is the Future," *Wall Street Journal,* June 3, 2013, http://online.wsj.com/article/SB10001424127887324659404578504761168566272.html.

61 Nathan Heller, "Laptop U," *New Yorker,* May 20, 2013, http://www.newyorker.com/reporting/2013/05/20/130520fa_fact_heller?currentPage=all.

62 Zachary Karabell, "College Is Going Online, Whether We Like It or Not," *The Atlantic,* May 17, 2013, http://www.theatlantic.com/business/archive/2013/05/college-is-going-online-whether-we-like-it-or-not/275976/.

63 *Id.*

64 Guilbert Brown, "Making Higher Education an Open Book," Pope Center Commentaries, February 13, 2008, http://www.popecenter.org/commentaries/article.html?id=1963.

65 U.S. Census Bureau, "After a Recent Upswing, College Enrollment Declines, Census Bureau Reports," September 3, 2013, http://www.census.gov/newsroom/releases/archives/education/cb13-153.html.

EDUCATION

1 Terence P. Jeffrey, "Two-Thirds of Wisconsin Public-School 8th Graders Can't Read Proficiently – Despite Highest Per Pupil Spending in Midwest," CNS News, February 11, 2011, http://cnsnews.com/news/article/two-thirds-wisconsin-public-school-8th-graders-can-t-read-proficiently-despite-highest.

2 Seth Godin, *Stop Stealing Dreams (What Is School For?),* 10–11, www.sethgodin.com/sg/docs/stopstealingdreamsscreen.pdf.

3 The National Commission on Excellence in Education, *A Nation at Risk* (1983), 9, http://datacenter.spps.org/uploads/SOTW_A_Nation_at_Risk_1983.pdf.

4 John Hicks, "Annual Survey of Economic Theory: The Theory of Monopoly," *3 Econometrica 1* (1935), 8.

5 The National Commission on Excellence in Education, *A Nation at Risk,* 9.

6 Thomas Hine, "The Rise and Fall of the Teenager," *American Heri-*

tage, September 1999, http://web.archive.org/web/20010306124204/www.americanheritage.com/99/sep/070e.htm.

7   Joseph Allen and Claudia Worrell, *Escaping the Endless Adolescence: How We Can Help Our Teenagers Grow Up Before They Grow Old* (2009).

8   Allen and Worrell, 8.

9   Allen and Worrell, 107–108.

10 Allen and Worrell, 108.

11 Robert Epstein, *The Case Against Adolescence: Rediscovering the Adult in Every Teen* (2007), 24. The paper-route point is on 33.

12 Epstein, 286.

13 Amber Winkler and Daniela Fairchild, "The School Staffing Surge: Decades of Employment Growth in America's Public Schools," Education Gadfly, October 25, 2012, http://www.edexcellence.net/commentary/education-gadfly-weekly/2012/october-25/the-school-staffing-surge.html.

14 Robert Maranto and Michael McShane, "5 Myths About Education," *Philadelphia Inquirer,* October 19, 2012, http://articles.philly.com/2012-10-19/ news/34557060_1_education-myths-charter-schools-public-schools.

15 Motoko Rich, "Enrollment Off in Big Districts, Forcing Layoffs," *The New York Times,* July 24, 2012, http://www.nytimes.com/2012/07/24/education/largest-school-districts-see-steady-drop-in-enrollment.html?_r=0.

16 Ovetta Wiggins, "Middle Class Parents Closely Watching Changes In Prince George's Public Schools," *Washington Post,* May 26, 2013, http://www.washingtonpost.com/local/education/middle-class-parents-closely-watching-changes-in-prince-georges-public-schools/2013/05/26/1d21d492-c330-11e2-914f-a7aba60512a7_story.html.

17 *Buffy the Vampire Slayer,* "Dead Man's Party," available at http://www.buffyguide.com/episodes/deadmans/deadmansquotes.shtml

18 Lauren Keiper, "Home Schooling Grows More Popular in America," *Huffington Post,* May 25, 2011, http://www.huffingtonpost.com/2011/03/16/home-schooling-mainstream_n_836591.html. ("Once considered distinctly Christian, the movement is deepening its mainstream roots, experts say.")

19 Paul Elie, "The Homeschool Diaries: In New York City, Teaching Your Own Kids Can Make the Most Practical Sense," *The Atlantic,* September 19, 2012, http://www.theatlantic.com/magazine/archive/2012/10/the-homeschool-diaries/309089/#.UORwkji8Nbo.facebook.

20 *Id.*

21 "Fast Facts About Online Learning," International Association for K-12 Online Learning, http://web.archive.org/web/20121030145435/http://www.inacol.org/press/docs/nacol_fast_facts.pdf.

22 That's the short version. Disappointingly, Kaplan College Prep sold out to another online company, K12.com, whose offerings weren't as good for her. She wound up finishing at Laurel Springs High School, a California online school catering to child stars and athletes (Elijah Wood and Hayden Panettiere are alumni), which was okay, but not quite as well suited for her as Kaplan. Meanwhile after a year of engineering, despite having a 4.0, she decided that engineering wasn't for her and has moved on to an inexpensive but excellent state university honors program. But as I told her, when you graduate from high school at 16, you're allowed to change your mind. And, thanks to her early graduation, she's still likely to finish college sooner than most of her peers.

23 Jenna Wortham and Nick Bilton, "Before Tumblr, Founder Made Mom Proud. He Quit School," *New York Times,* May 21, 2012, http://www.nytimes.com/2013/05/21/technology/david-karp-quit-school-to-get-serious-about-start-ups.html?pagewanted=all&_r=0.

SOME QUASI-PREDICTIONS

1 James Dunnigan, "Troops Game Their Way out of Ambushes," *StrategyPage*, July 5, 2004, http://www.strategypage.com/dls/articles2004/200475.asp.

2 Frank Vizard, "Couch to Combat: A popular computer game called 'America's Army' has evolved into a high-tech tool for training today's soldiers," *Popular Mechanics* (June 2005), 80.

3 Dan Nosowitz, "9 Percent of Americans Say They'd Bonk a Sexbot," *Popular Science,* April 11, 2013, http://www.popsci.com/technology/article/2013-04/9-percent-americans-polled-say-theyd-bonk-sexbot.

SOME CONCLUDING THOUGHTS

1 Arthur Allen Leff, "Economic Analysis of Law: Some Realism About Nominalism," *60 Va. L. Rev.* (1974), 451, 469, http://digitalcommons.law.yale.edu/cgi/viewcontent.cgi?article=3816&context=fss_papers.

2 J. R. Hicks, "Annual Survey of Economic Theory: The Theory of Monopoly," *3 Econometrica 1* (1935), 8.

3 In the words of Dan Aykroyd's character in *Ghostbusters*, Dr. Roy Stantz, "Personally, I liked the university. They gave us money and facilities, we didn't have to produce anything! You've never been out of college! You don't know what it's like out there! I've *worked* in the private sec-

tor. They expect *results*." Available at http://www.imdb.com/title/
tt0087332/quotes?ref_=tt_ql_3.

4 Daniel Pink, *Drive* (2009), 86–108.

5 Paul Krugman, "Sympathy for the Luddites," *New York Times*, June 14,
2013,http://www.nytimes.com/2013/06/14/opinion/krugman-sympathy-
for-the-luddites.html?ref=opinion.

INDEX

Page numbers followed by n and nn indicate notes.
Italicized page numbers refer to figures and tables.

A NOTE ON THE TYPE

The New School has been set in Walbaum 2010, a family of types created by František Štorm following the models of the nineteenth-century German typographer Justus Erich Walbaum. Derived in large part from the example of Giambattista Bodoni's types, Walbaum maintains the dramatic contrast of thick and thin strokes characteristic of so-called modern types, but is distinguished by its broader set width and taller lower-case letters. These characteristics make Walbaum a type better suited to longer texts and smaller sizes than the too-elegant Bodoni – or its dazzling French cousin, Didot. The present types, available in a standard-height version and an "XL" version with a still-higher x-height, are intended address the defects present in the original types (and in later interpretations) and to expand the usefulness of these hard-working types. As Štorm wrote when he began digitizing the types in 2002, "The expression of the type face is robust, as if it had been seasoned with the spicy smell of the dung of Saxon cows somewhere near Weimar, where [Walbaum] had his type foundry in the years 1803–39."

DESIGN & COMPOSITION BY CARL W. SCARBROUGH